THE MAKING OF BLACK LIVES MATTER

THE MAKING OF
BLACK LIVES MATTER

A Brief History of an Idea

UPDATED EDITION

CHRISTOPHER J. LEBRON

OXFORD

UNIVERSITY PRESS

Oxford University Press is a department of the University of Oxford. It furthers
the University's objective of excellence in research, scholarship, and education
by publishing worldwide. Oxford is a registered trade mark of Oxford University
Press in the UK and certain other countries.

Published in the United States of America by Oxford University Press
198 Madison Avenue, New York, NY 10016, United States of America.

Library of Congress Cataloging-in-Publication Data
Names: Lebron, Christopher J., author.
Title: The making of Black Lives Matter : a brief history of an idea /
Christopher J. Lebron.
Description: Updated edition. | New York, NY : Oxford University Press, [2023] |
Includes bibliographical references and index.
Identifiers: LCCN 2022059881 (print) | LCCN 2022059882 (ebook) |
ISBN 9780197577356 (pb) | ISBN 9780197577349 (hb) |
ISBN 9780197577370 (epub)
Subjects: LCSH: Black lives matter movement. | African Americans—Social
conditions—21st century. | African Americans—Politics and government—
21st century. | Equality—United States. | Racism—United States. |
United States—Race relations.
Classification: LCC E185.615.L393 2023 (print) | LCC E185.615 (ebook) |
DDC 305.896/0730905—dc23/eng/20221220
LC record available at https://lccn.loc.gov/2022059881
LC ebook record available at https://lccn.loc.gov/2022059882

DOI: 10.1093/oso/9780197577349.001.0001

Paperback printed by Sheridan Books, Inc., United States of America
Hardback printed by Bridgeport National Bindery, Inc., United States of America

"People can't, unhappily, invent their mooring posts, their lovers and their friends, anymore than they can invent their parents. Life gives these and also takes them away and the great difficulty is to say Yes to life."

— JAMES BALDWIN, *Giovanni's Room*

CONTENTS

INTRODUCTION TO

THE UPDATED EDITION

AN INTRODUCTION FOR THE SECOND edition of a book like *The Making of Black Lives Matter: A Brief History of an Idea* is a less straightforward thing than it might first seem. Typically, when an author revisits a book some years later, their ruminations center on how they may have become clearer on the ideas in their book, taken into consideration critical corrections, or, maybe, generally how their own thinking has matured thanks to the miracle of living a life. But as I sit here, toward the end of 2021, experiencing a late fall in which the leaves seem to refuse to quit the trees, I am reflecting in the midst of an entirely different set of considerations.

As the first edition of this book was going to press, an unapologetic racist, misogynist, homophobe, and xeno-phobe had slid through the safeguards of democracy meant to keep people of low morals out of the most powerful position in the world. Some thought, sure, Donald Trump won the Electoral College vote (even as he lost the popular vote), but the structure of major institutions would train? coerce? persuade? such a man to become a proper president, a responsible custodian of all Americans' welfare. But you cannot train a person who denies the power of knowledge, cannot coerce a bully, cannot persuade someone motivated by irrational animus toward anyone who disagrees with them. And then, as if the real erosion of what passes for democracy in America in the face of clumsy, intellectually bereft demagoguery were not a historical emergency all on its own, the globe was beset by a life-threatening pandemic three years later. COVID-19 took nearly one million American lives as the same president suggested we inject ourselves with bleach, while declaring that science had no more idea of what was happening than the average person on the street; indeed the bare idea of wearing a slim piece of cloth over one's mouth to protect others from a deadly disease was enough to enrage him and his quite substantial and immovable base.

In the midst of this most recent catastrophe, America was reminded that blacks have been suffering catastrophe since we were dragged to North America. In the summer of 2020 another police officer with no patience for the idea of black humanity casually placed his knee on another black man's neck while looking at the surrounding crowd, befuddled that anyone could disapprove of casual racial murder in public. Under that knee George Floyd took his last breath, and America held its own. Because this time was different. We had all been forced into varying states of idleness in the midst of two horrors—the Trump presidency and the

COVID-19 pandemic—and this last horror, this public execution seemed one too many traumas for us to process. The nation erupted in widespread angry protest. Importantly, white Americans turned out in record numbers supporting the movement and/or the idea Black Lives Matter. It seemed we were at a turning point. It seemed as if white Americans finally—finally!—got it.

Except, not really. Soon what had first appeared to be unalloyed white support for black lives became something of a spectacle centering on white and other nonblack protesters as they complained of various indignities, co-opting media attention in the process. The case of "Naked Athena" is an example that is as astounding as it is baffling. Athena, an apparently white protestor (though someone claiming later to be "Athena" described herself simply as "nonblack") positioned herself naked, legs splayed, sitting on a street in Portland, Oregon, during the protests in an area occupied by police. Her reason, according to the person claiming to be Athena: "My message . . . other than my feminine response of wanting to show them what my version of vulnerability looks like . . . was we're all out here, these protesters, [and] the only thing we have in common is, we have masks on and we're out here at night."[1] A statement I am sure George Floyd's family would have a hard time endorsing.

And then public opinion support for Black Lives Matter, which had been at an all-time high when the protests began immediately following Floyd's murder, plummeted from a high of 52 percent of respondents to 43 percent.[2] Commentators began to reasonably suggest that a lot of white support was in part a function of COVID boredom: white Americans had seen a horrific thing with not much else going on in their COVID-isolated lives and, without a job to go to or the ability to see friends otherwise, took to the streets. But the solidarity was somewhat illusory. Undoubtedly a lot of these people were genuinely upset at what they saw on that TV or computer screen, but under any other circumstances they would have *merely* been troubled, and their lives would have gone uninterrupted. But during the height of the pandemic, neighbors who had never once mentioned to me a concern for racial justice were enthusiastically recounting their participation in a recent local march and planning on how to avoid contracting COVID while participating in the next. Since then, however, with the world hobbling toward normalcy and Trump out of office, I've yet to hear one of them say another word about racial justice or see any one of them take a civic-minded action in support of black lives mattering. The style has passed, though many "Black Lives Matter" lawn signs persist, sun-bleached and fading.

The past four years have taught two exceedingly important lessons with which anyone truly concerned with black life mattering must seriously contend.

First, the rise and staying power of Donald Trump's racial nationalism indicates not something wrong with him (which surely there is, at least with his morals, in any case) but with this nation. As became increasingly common to note, Trump was a symptom, not a cause of this nation's tragically anemic inability to reliably and robustly express concern for nonwhite citizens, especially those not straight and male. Trump roused a large and enduring portion of the electorate, barely bothering to veil that with him at the lead, the nonsense of showing compassion to blacks, women, queers, immigrants, non-Christians would come to an end. Trump did not create these beliefs. His only innovation was a market one: who else was out there as a national politician unapologetically courting resentful whites and making it sound like this made him the greatest American patriot of the twenty-first century? Very few. Trump, with not much to lose, simply removed the veneer of coded language from Republican politics and injected them with righteous fury. A hateful political star was born on the winds of that which was blowing through America for the past four centuries: racial fear and resentment.

Second, what is the true state of our nation's commitment to systemic racial change beyond the difficulties the far- and alt-right present? In concordance with the largest amount of white support for racial justice the nation has ever seen, radical institutional solutions seemed truly possible. Prominent among these was the call to "Defund the Police." This slogan was less fortunate than "Black Lives Matter" for it seemed a blanket brute force call for simply getting rid of police, when, in fact, there were more practical and elegant proposals as part of the movement, such as redirecting funds to positively diversify police and civic resources. For example, if today you were to notice a homeless individual acting erratically, it is likely that the first line of encounter such a person would be with armed law enforcement rather than a trained mental health professional whose first and main aim is to de-escalate without presenting a mortal threat. Such legislation promised to humanize public safety and made it on to some major state house legislative agendas, only to mostly fizzle at the same time as popular white support for Black Lives Matter. Crucially, such deflated ambition not only calls into question who we are as a nation but asks, realistically, what are our possibilities to be greater than we have ever been on the count of racial justice? This general phenomenon is the flip-side problem of Trump having merely been a symptom of our nation's worst vices. The answers have been less heartening than hoped, especially once one considers that our democratic savior from Donald Trump, Joe Biden, was himself directly responsible for the 1994 Crime Bill. This legislation was instrumental in the expansion of police presence, power, and resources that has led to all the black deaths we mourn today and will, in all likelihood, continue to mourn until we achieve—if we can achieve—our better selves.

***

It is with these thoughts in mind that I offer a framing for the new chapter that is now a part of *The Making of Black Lives Matter*. When I wrote the first edition of this book, I was keen to enter the conversation of the movement on an intellectual level, and that presented certain considerations for the book's scope. My one lingering question for the book was, what if I extended the story of the intellectual girding of Black Lives Matter into the Black Power era? As it stood, the book's journey ended in an important but also orthodox, maybe even predictable moment with James Baldwin and Martin Luther King Jr. In one sense, this was fitting as it closed out, on a more positive note, the civil rights trajectory that began in the book with Frederick Douglass and Ida B. Wells. But in another sense, this left readers in an inconvenient place because crucial questions arose right after Baldwin and King's moment, precisely because there was a kind of backlash to civil rights from both white institutions that reinvented modes of domination, for example, the modern rise of a very robust police state, and from black activists who maintained, following the temperamental lead of Malcolm X, that the civil rights victories were thin and the movement required more radical propositions. While blacks could vote, they could also be beat by the police more, and while there was (some) integration, black was still not beautiful or "proud." Thus, the late 1960s into the 1970s gave rise to the Black Power movement in all its manifestation: black arts, the reclamation of African-inspired aesthetic, and so on. There were important lessons to be drawn that did not make it into the first book, but what would I do now with a chance to make this contribution in a second edition?

The answer was to work from the core of Black Power concerns, but this time making less obvious yet no less foundational choices in my conversation partners. The "obvious" subjects for such a chapter would have been Huey P. Newton and the Black Panther Party for Self-Defense, along with Kwame Ture/Stokely Carmichael. But that choice introduced challenges of its own. First, and importantly, it threatened to problematically disrupt the gender balance I had worked to establish in the first edition. A very reasonable objection to the Panthers was their strong commitment, explicitly and implicitly, to masculine ideals of leadership and attitudes for most of the party's brief existence. And then if I paired them with Ture, that would have made the issue of gender balance even more tenuous. Thus, I chose the pairing of Angela Davis and Amiri Baraka. I want to say a few words on why I chose them, the challenges they present, and then, ultimately, the powerful contributions they make in considering the matter of black lives in a post-Trump America.

There are three reasons for choosing Davis and Baraka. First, in important ways, they mirror each other. Their lives and activism overlap historically; thus they were responding to very similar, sometimes the very same events in their writings, but from their distinctive vantage points. For example, while Davis, on the West Coast, was confronting the Soledad Brothers trial and threats from rival factions within the West Coast Black Power movement, Baraka was dealing with the reverberations of those rivalries as he sought to build robust black institutions in Newark, New Jersey, in hopes of shaping a mayoral race. Second, both thinkers left copious writings—this is a deeply important factor when covering the ideas of historical figures. It makes tracing the core concerns in their thinking and activism as well as their maturation over time much easier and precise. That said, in the case of Davis and Baraka, there is more work than can be attended to in one brief chapter, which leads to the third reason they make a great pairing: they had complementary views and deep interests on the relationship between jazz as a black art form and the political valences of black life. I will have more to say about this below.

It is worth noting some challenges in dealing with the work and lives of Davis and Baraka. For Davis, the conceptual depth as well as analytic consistency of her work is of varying quality, spanning a significant range of time as well as subject matter. A virtue of her early work is that her training as a philosopher shows through with a fair amount of consistency, making her earlier work more reflective and probing in ways her later work does not quite match, and this is not an insignificant concern for a book of this nature. Baraka presents more substantial challenges. He had problematic views concerning gender and homosexuality. In predictable ways, he mirrors a very black-masculinist view common to prominent male participants in the Black Power movement. He seems to have become more recalcitrant and softer in these views in his later life. This is unfortunate because it is his earliest work which, ironically, is most useful for us. No apology can or should be made on Baraka's behalf. Yet, at the same time, I want to resist the recent trend in throwing out the thinking we like with the thinker we don't. We can find value in writings that exceed the personality in question, and that is what I intend on doing; we need not accept homophobia or misogyny to appreciate the power of reclaiming certain readings of the history of black art that point the way toward cultural emancipation. And that is what I intend on doing.

This brings us to their contributions. One understanding of "black lives matter" is a slightly conservative one where the demand is simply that whites acknowledge that black lives matter. But there is more to it than this. The slogan is also meant to be transformative of a nation and its citizens who benefit regularly from white privilege and/or practice or embrace or passively accept white supremacy. But "black lives matter" is also an inflection point for black Americans, a way of dealing with the age-old problem of figuring out what it means to black or brown in America. Such questions center the theme of becoming. What are the imaginative horizons for creating a self? What resources are available to black and brown Americans? What limits and obstacles seem to exist? How do we push past those limits and remove those obstacles? These questions introduce a deeply emancipatory program into blacks' lives so long as there is an attendant consciousness. This is where Davis and Baraka are helpful.

Both Davis and Baraka grew up in mid-century America where antiblack violence was common, but also, on the horizon, were those fighting and slowly proving that whites did not need to hold, in fact had no right in determining the possibilities of black life. Both Davis and Baraka bore witness to and were victims of racial violence, including from police. Both bore witness to the immediate aftermath of the cultural epoch of the Harlem Renaissance, and both were present for important amendments to that moment. Significantly, for Davis and Baraka, in their distinct but closely related ways, the blues and jazz were art forms that spoke without apology to the theme of becoming. As I shall discuss in the chapter, both saw the blues and jazz as not only the rightful cultural heritage of black Americans but as an art form that was born of a particular sociopolitical existence, beginning in slavery and evolving to meet the times of a Jim Crow—and, later, a post–civil rights—America. The blues, as Langston Hughes intimates in chapter 2, was a politically expressive art form, and as Davis puts it in *Blues Legacies and Black Feminism*, "Emerging during the decades following the abolition of slavery, the blues gave musical expression to the new social and sexual realities encountered by African Americans as free women and men." Blues was a genre that seemed to anticipate an era when blacks could express full civic autonomy, by first suggesting full personal autonomy in the music. As we will see, Davis properly credits black women blues artists with leading the charge into the American imagination through the power of their artistic vision combined with the unapologetic manner in which they owned their womanhood, sexuality, and blackness. Baraka's story of the blues delves into a different aspect of black history and is more archaeological, as it were, in its statement of the relationship between the blues as a living artifact of African culture and American blackness. In *Blues People*, he writes, "Blues did begin in slavery, and it is from that 'peculiar institution' . . . that blues did find its particular form. And if slavery dictated certain aspects of blues form and content, so did the so-called Emancipation and its subsequent problems dictate the path the blues would take."

Despite their distinctive emphases. Davis and Baraka each, in their own way, motivate what I want to suggest is a fitting closing thought for this volume: What should be the stance of black Americans toward themselves as well as toward the nation as we consider whether America can and will ever become the version of itself imagined by the founders? Through their readings of blues and jazz, which inform their own activism and writing on prison abolition and community organizing, Davis's and Baraka's answer seems to be this: we should not seek to be great Americans but rather seek to become free people in the deepest sense, despite America, not because of America. And in doing so, yes, we help America achieve its best self, but we ensure that we become proper selves in the first place as we come to possess our humanity and embrace resistance to any threat to that humanity. Davis writes, "The first condition of freedom is the open act of resistance." The Black Lives Matter movement has taken this sensibility to heart. Between the date of the original publication of this book and the time of this writing, the list of unarmed blacks killed by police and civilians has only continued to grow. We can honor the fallen dead with memories. But the way to honor the living is through resistance so that future generations can possess memories free from unnecessary tragedy. This is the new American dream.

INTRODUCTION TO THE FIRST

EDITION: NAMING THE DEAD IN

THE NAME OF THE LIVING

IT CAN BE DIFFICULT TO keep up. I've published one previous book, numerous papers, essays, and book reviews in a wide range of outlets, both academic and public, and have another book manuscript well in the making. And every time, I begin at the beginning—I always write an introduction first. The introduction is what has typically guided the vision and framework for whatever follows: op-ed, essay, book review, book. That has been my own conventional wisdom. When I began work on *The Making of Black Lives Matter: A Brief History of an Idea*, I knew I couldn't write that way. Though this is a book of intellectual history, its motivating moment is a dynamic one. I hoped beyond hope that in the year or so it took me to write it, the fatal conditions in America that moved me to write the book in the first place would allow me to qualify with a ray of optimism the somber reflections that follow. But I also knew that things might change very little, or possibly get worse. I intentionally saved the introduction as the last major piece of writing for this book. The result? Just one week prior to my sitting at my computer to write these words, Alton Sterling and Philando Castile were killed by Baton Rouge and Minneapolis police, respectively. We must add their names to the dead in the name of the living:

Oscar Grant, Shereese Francis, Rekia Boyd, Kendrec McDade, Tamon Robinson, Shantel Davis, Jonathan Ferrell, Jordan Baker, McKenzie Cochran, Eric Garner, John Crawford, Michael Brown, Tanisha Anderson, Ezell Ford, Kajieme Powell, Akai Gurley, Tamir Rice, Dontre Hamilton, Bettie Jones, Roy Nelson, Tiara Thomas, Alonzo Smith, Anthony Ashford, Tyree Crawford, Samuel Dubose, Sandra Bland, Walter Scott, Natasha McKenna, Alton Sterling, Philando Castile.

This list is far from complete. In fact, it's short by hundreds of names that are the damning evidence of the level of violence against black bodies in America. What you might find shocking is that the hundreds of names missing do not span a century or even decades of American history. Rather, the list I've provided begins in 2012. And it is missing the one name we might look back upon from some future vantage point as the most important in the history of today's racial struggle: Trayvon Martin.

The story of the movement that seeks to redeem a nation begins with Martin. The evening of February 26, 2012, Martin was walking through a Sanford, Florida community wearing a hoodie and holding only a soft drink and some candy. George Zimmerman, a neighborhood watch volunteer, deemed Martin suspicious and called the police though Martin had not actually done anything actionable—his only possible crime seemed to be walking while black. Though advised by the 911 operator to stand down and keep his distance, Zimmerman initiated a confrontation that resulted in a scuffle that ended with him shooting seventeen-year-old Martin dead. Despite Martin's younger age, weight, and size disadvantage, and the all-important fact that he was unarmed, his character quickly became the center of speculation and conversation—he was a black teenager wearing a hoodie, walking through someone else's neighborhood; if Zimmerman suspected him, he must have been suspect-worthy. It came as a surprise to some in America when, in the summer of 2013, Zimmerman was found not guilty on all charges related to Martin's death. It was at this moment that Alicia Garza, Patrisse Cullors, and Opal Tometi made history. As Garza states on the website bearing the movement's name, "I created #BlackLivesMatter with Patrisse Cullors and Opal Tometi, two of my sisters, as a call to action for Black people after 17-year-old Trayvon Martin was posthumously placed on trial for his own murder and the killer, George Zimmerman, was not held accountable for the crime he committed."[1] Thus, it was the death and failure of our justice system to account for the unnecessary death of a black American that prompted three women to offer these three basic and urgent words to the American people: black lives matter.

Today, #BlackLivesMatter has become a force demanding change in America. Eschewing traditional hierarchical leadership models, the movement cannot be identified with any single leader or small group of leaders, despite the role Cullors, Tometi, and Garza played in giving us the social movement hashtag that will likely define our generation. Rather, #BlackLivesMatter represents an ideal that motivates, mobilizes, and informs the actions and programs of many local branches of the movement. Much like the way a corporate franchise works, minus revenue and profit,

#BlackLivesMatter is akin to a social movement brand that can be picked up and deployed by any interested group of activists inclined to speak out and act against racial injustice.

There is no doubt that the movement itself is historically momentous, even if it remains unclear as of this writing the level of policy efficacy #BlackLivesMatter has been able to bring to bear on the problem of racial justice. Indeed, it is precisely because of the nascent and formative status that I resisted writing directly on the movement. I did not, nor do not as of this writing perceive a space or opportunity to say something sufficiently systematic and helpful about the movement on which so many black Americans are pinning their hopes. Yet, there is something undeniably powerful about those three words: black lives matter. Yes, it is true that they were brought into our political existence at a moment marked by tragedy and unjustifiable losses of black life. That alone makes those three words a touchstone for our American lives today—the struggle to insist that black lives are indeed lives and therefore not candidates for cursory or careless or hateful or negligible elimination. The problem as I saw it from the perspectives of a citizen, a black Latino man, and a scholar was to honor the moment in which we find ourselves, at the helm of which is a movement that seeks to finally undo this nation's murderous racial history. This is a history that spans and reaches like a weed across centuries. Indeed, the only way, I think, to appropriately reflect on this moment that seeks once and for all to place black Americans on a level of human equality with whites is to treat the #BlackLivesMatter movement as intelligent, enduring, and politically savvy. As a trained political philosopher, I had no way of directly engaging the movement given its short life. The Black Power generation had in the sharp and brave tome penned by Kwame Ture and Charles Hamilton, *Black Power*, a published manifesto and theoretical edifice. In contrast, no such text exists to provide the philosophical moorings of #BlackLivesMatter.

This realization provides the central aim of this book. As I had turned those three words over in my mind—black lives matter—and read them in news stories and heard them spoken by commentators and friends, it became clear the three words themselves, as distinct from the particular strategies and agents of the movement, indicated a sentiment that was as old as the desire to be free from slavery. From the point of view of my own professional training, "black lives matter" represents a civic desire for equality and a human desire for respect, the intellectual roots of which lie deep in the history of black American thought. And precisely because the history is rich and established, I perceived an opportunity to contribute to our moment by bringing to bear the forefathers and foremothers of black American social and political thought on an urgent claim: that black Americans are humans, too. Precisely because blacks' struggle for human acknowledgment is centuries old, what can those who have been on the front lines in the past teach us about our present ideas about the struggle? Indeed, since the struggle is as old as America itself, are we equipped with the right kind of ethos to make our present-day social movements as effective as they can and need to be?

To attempt to begin to answer this question I sought out a select number of thinkers in the history of black intellectual life. You need to know up front that contrary to academic pretensions, there was no systematic parsing of the vast number of options of important contributors to the black intellectual tradition. American intellectual life has been blessed with the gift of the deep well of black imagination, analysis, arts, and letters that is our inheritance today. No justice could be done to the tradition in so slim a volume as this. Thus, my criteria were different, personal as well as intellectual—when I reflected on my own pain, anxiety, fears, and hopes, who were the forefathers and foremothers whose words provided inspiration and insight, whose writing and ideas counseled me best in dealing with the injustice that comes with living in this brown skin? The collection of thinkers I engage in this text represents a range of powerful insights that do not exhaust our intellectual options. Rather, they provide a critical initial starting place in coming to terms with the relationship between black thought and black American politics and life.

The Making of Black Lives Matter: A Brief History of An Idea suggests a political agenda as well as the outlining of a philosophical system. When I initially undertook the project you hold in your hand as a completed book, my plan was modest—to engage a small group of very important thinkers in the black thought tradition. "Black lives matter" are three words often used as a lament, as a signal that our democracy has been, is, and seems likely to continue failing 12 percent of its population. The movement exists because many feel, believe, and hope that the past is not necessarily an augur of the future, that the arc of the universe does bend toward justice, and that good and conscientious people might sharpen that trajectory before many more black lives are lost or ruined. In the pages that follow, I provide an essential window into a strand of black American social and political thought that can help provide some of the intellectual and philosophical moorings we need to fully appreciate the depth of "black lives matter."

America was at a crucial junction in the middle of the nineteenth century. The institution of slavery had been the backbone of the nation's social order and economic logic, yet it was coming under increasing pressure from abolitionists, who tirelessly pressed slave owners and non-slave-owning observers of the institution to accept that America was involved in a great crime against humanity. Moreover, abolitionists defiantly argued that slavery betrayed the very ideals of America's democratic founding. Into this scene stepped the self-emancipated Frederick Douglass. Douglass's charge, as he saw it, was to bring the perspective of servitude and inhumane suffering to the American people and compel them to confront the hypocrisy of their political associations and institutions. As slavery died, a virulent form of white supremacy moved to fill the void emancipation had left in America's racial power structure. Jim Crow was a social system of segregation and subordination. At its least malignant it advocated for the principle of separate but equal accommodations for white and black Americans. But the very minimal moral embodied in even that principle was a sham. Rather, the great sin of Jim Crow was lynching—the murderous license white Americans exercised in extrajudicially terrorizing and executing black Americans. Ida B. Wells, after having been forced to flee her hometown under threat of violent retribution for exposing lynching, developed into a great American journalist and activist. In the span of a handful of years of observing the deficiencies in both our laws and media coverage of white terrorism against blacks, Wells became and remained into the twentieth century America's leading voice against white America's murderous predilections. Douglass's and Wells's struggles and ideas are our first engagement with the history of the idea "black lives matter" in chapter 1.

Black art has always been and remains a pillar of black political expression. Though widely derided among conservative whites and even some blacks, gangster rap like that produced by the west coast group N.W.A. has as part of its roots statements against police brutality. Chapter 2 acknowledges the present uses of black urban performance to make a stand for social progress, and then goes back to a foundational moment in black arts and letters—the Harlem Renaissance. This engagement is challenging. In the Harlem Renaissance, also known as the era of the New Negro, we have a truly fresh and transformative historical moment with a great many players overlapping, interacting, collaborating, disagreeing, competing to define the future of American democracy through artistic expression. We engage just two important figures. The first, Langston Hughes, was present at the beginning of the movement Alain Locke helped to initiate. Through his poetry and essays he resisted the elitism that sometimes threatened to and did at times define the Renaissance. Hughes's work is deeply important for democratic thinking given his allegiance to the beat, cadence, and texture of the lives of everyday "low down" folk, as he admiringly rather than disdainfully called them. In this regard, Zora Neale Hurston is the second important partner in the chapter's conversation. She, like Hughes, affirmed the value of common and mundane experiences, such as setting out for a day of work at the railroad. Similarly, Hurston championed the importance of black women's expressive capacities in both intellectual and artistic life. This combination of commitments urged Hurston in the direction of cataloguing and performing black folklore in service to excavating the voice of black Americans. For Hurston, black life mattered in part because it served as an ongoing chronicle of the modes of personal and civic engagement black people employed in refusing to be completely determined by oppression.

Chapter 3 centers on the issues of gender and sexuality in black equality. While the death of black men like Trayvon Martin, Michael Brown, and Philando Castile have gotten a fair share of media coverage, the struggle black women have faced across centuries against rape, oppression from white men and women and black men, as well as death at the hands of the state has received inadequate attention. Similarly, some of our most important black women thinkers have not received their due as canonical contributors to black American thought. Here we enter into conversation first with Anna Julia Cooper, a civic and educational leader at the turn of the nineteenth century widely considered to be the first black feminist. She spent a lifetime arguing for the fundamental importance of black women's equality in the struggle for racial equality more generally. Cooper argued that the structure of women's oppression could be and should be used as a blueprint for a much more rigorous quest for an egalitarian society both within the black community and between blacks and whites. Audre Lorde enters our picture as a more contemporary continuation of Cooper's arguments and struggle. Lorde in particular extends Cooper's concerns to offer a richer and more robust framework of socially salient and politically relevant identity. As a woman who spent her life defending the many identities she claimed for herself—black, woman, lesbian, poet, activist, mother— Lorde believed it was crucial that wider society appreciate and learn how complicated and burdened a life can become when each of one's many identities is constantly weighed down by oppression. Additionally, Lorde, more than Cooper (who considered herself a proper southern woman), bravely educated readers on the political relevance of erotic life, longing, and loving to the struggle for racial equality. In doing so, Lorde left us an important strand of thought for our moment today in which we collectively continue to struggle to fully acknowledge the suffering and struggles of women and members of the black LGBT community.

Resentment against historical white supremacy and contemporary white privilege is easy to understand given how systems of racial ignorance continuously work to undermine black flourishing. In the course of black social movements and thought, more militant mindsets, such as that articulated by the Black Panthers, have vied for the hearts and minds of black Americans. These movements and philosophies have framed America as irredeemably corrupted by the history of white supremacy. This corruption, in the view of militants, is fated to disrupt any attempts at reasonable discourse to secure blacks' equality. Thus, equality must be secured by blacks distrusting whites and taking their security into their own hands, by force if necessary. A cursory survey of our racial history reveals how legitimate frustrations and fears can lead to militancy. It was then all the more remarkable that love, the subject of chapter 4, was so important to some thinkers at the time. James Baldwin, maybe one of America's most perceptive and sensitive twentieth-century essayists, counseled love as a guiding ethic in black life. This is especially remarkable given Baldwin's very intense anger toward white America. But Baldwin turned this anger into an ethical fuel to hold on to his own humanity. He counseled blacks to love themselves on account of the humanity no white person could ever deny them; he counseled blacks to love whites in order to redeem the humanity whites were in danger of forfeiting by virtue of their complicity in the great injustices blacks suffered. Martin Luther King Jr. also counseled an ethics based on love, but it was one both more sterile and more philosophically rigorous. Whereas Baldwin had some faith in the human intuition for *philial*—or kinship—love, King, a seminary-trained scholar and preacher, synthesized a more systematic morality with *agape*, or disinterested, love. Consonant with the teaching of enlightenment-era German moral theorist Immanuel Kant, King felt that we had ethical duties we could not abandon willfully. Of these was the duty to love others out of respect for the fact that all are beings capable of leading morally upright lives. Despite its cooler nature, King's love ethic gave rise to a crucial moment in the struggle for civil rights. The use of nonviolent protest as a cornerstone for national moral progress remains one of King's enduring contributions to American society, and it was grounded in the notion of love.

It might have been enough for us to consider the work and lives of these eight thinkers in light of our present moment. But I press a bit further in the final chapter. This book ends on a note more critical and editorial than the previous chapters, for there is another point that needs to be made. We must appreciate that #BlackLivesMatter became a necessary movement not during the years of Jim Crow lynching or the uncertain years of the civil rights movement, when it was unclear that blacks would ever secure formal equality. Rather, black Americans have felt compelled to take to the streets to combat rampant institutional inequality and police brutality well into the twenty-first century, more than fifty years after Martin Luther King Jr. helped pressure President Lyndon B. Johnson into moving the Civil Rights Act of 1964 through a recalcitrant Congress. It is my contention that what is needed today is a reconceptualization of radical ethics for black politics.

When we think of radical political ethics we tend to conflate that idea with militancy or violence. Indeed, a central argument of this book is that the thinkers we consider, from Douglass to Lorde to Hurston to King, were in fact radical thinkers. By this I mean something clear and basic—they were thinkers and activists who sought to establish for themselves an authority to protect black lives that was not openly given them by our society; and indeed, the authority to seek security was often withheld. Radicalism is the imagination and will to think and act outside the bounds of the normally acceptable. Yes, that can be achieved by wielding an AK-47 assault rifle in public as protection from an oppressive police force. It can also be achieved when Audre Lorde insists that erotic lesbian love is politically essential to her as a means of exercising her freedom and flexing her capacity for critical social judgment. In this final chapter, I synthesize from each previous chapter a radical lesson I hope can be found useful in the present-day American struggle for basic black well-being.

From our engagement with Frederick Douglass and Ida B. Wells I offer the lesson of *shameful publicity*. As both these thinkers fought for recognition and an end to state-permitted murder, they bypassed the norms of a conventional public to not only indict Americans but to force them to confront the slippage between their professed ideals and the horrendous treatment blacks endured. Hughes and Hurston expand the boundaries of resistance by insisting that blacks' acceptance by white Americans depended on more than rational moral argumentation but a kind of *countercolonization of the white imagination.* Cooper and Lorde teach us the lesson of *unconditional self-possession.* Each of these women left for black Americans of both genders and all sexual identities blueprints for refusing to negotiate one's self worth and for fully embracing the political possibilities our identities open for us. Finally, from Baldwin and King, we get a final step—the call to an ethos that embodies intelligent vulnerability but militant self-respect, what I call *unfragmented compassion.* Both men's commitment to the love ethic requires blacks risking what comfort and safety they can secure in order to build a stronger polity. They also draw a line of impenetrable resistance around their ideas of self-worth, thereby taking possession of something white Americans often assume they have influence over—blacks' self-respect and potential for flourishing. Taken together, our eight thinkers recommend a political ethical comportment to America that suggests an endorsement of the ideal of democracy while soundly and roundly rejecting the distortions and corruptions of *American* democracy without compromise—black humanity will be respected or blacks will no longer endorse the centuries-old asymmetrical project Audre Lorde famously spelled as "america" to demote the idea from grandness and properness to an immature and unformed state of a union. In doing so, a greater humanity will be displayed in holding white Americans close to the heart of racial justice that beats within black Americans.

As with all arguments, mine benefits most from foils. In this regard my choice may be surprising—black conservative-minded public intellectuals. I have chosen to confront one such thinker in the course of offering each radical lesson for a very straightforward reason—these thinkers have it as their mission to counsel blacks to be good and decent Americans based on hegemonic and lopsided standards of decency and respectability. They intend this counsel as a means to human flourishing despite the real and tragic obstacles blacks continue to face. I say, we need a more radical politics for a good and decent America before we can think justly about what it means for blacks to be good Americans. Part of insisting that black lives matter is also insisting that what's fair is fair.

AMERICAN SHAME AND

REAL FREEDOM

Oh! that the heart of this unbelieving nation could be
at once brought to a faith in the Eternal Laws
of justice, justice for all men, justice now and always,
justice without reservation or qualification
except those suggested by love and mercy.
—FREDERICK DOUGLASS, *"The Work of the Future"*

The South resented giving the Afro-American his freedom,
the ballot box, and the Civil Rights Law. The raids of the
Ku-Klux and White Liners to subvert reconstruction government,
the Hamburg and Ellerton, S.C., the Copiah County Miss.,
and the Lafayette Parish, La., massacres were excused as
the natural resentment of intelligence against government
by ignorance.
—IDA B. WELLS, *"The New Cry"*

THIS PUNCH WAS NOT LIKE other punches. John McGraw decided the black protester wasn't welcome in his space. He assaulted him then yelled, "The next time we see him, we might have to kill him." And Donald Trump was on the stage as this happened. The blow McGraw landed wasn't unique because it was a sucker punch. Many such punches have been thrown and have landed in the history of human fisti-cuffs. It wasn't wrong merely in its racist origins. Rather, it was awful and shameful because it was thrown by a white man at a black protester at a presidential rally for Donald Trump, who will surely go down in American history for shamelessly agitating for physical violence and discord in the name of American patriotism. In this regard, Trump is neither new nor original. What is shocking and galling is that in 2016 Trump and the culprit who landed the blow are able to operate with near impunity. Though the assaulter was eventually arrested, nothing has stopped Trump from reminding America, time and again, that the American way is both the racist and the violent way. But Trump does not stand alone. Indeed, the hashtag #BlackLivesMatter came into being in 2012, after Trayvon Martin was killed by a private citizen, who, like Trump, seemed to hold dear the halcyon days in America when violence was freely committed in the name of racism, against others deemed unworthy to occupy certain spaces or exercise certain liberties.

That blacks have consistently found themselves at the business end of whites' chains, ropes, fists, guns, and nooses is America's shame—our standards of equal liberty and protection under the law to which we, as a nation, claim to be committed, tend to falter and collapse when blacks depend on those standards and commitments. Slavery was an explicit practice of the ownership of black human bodies and the control of black lives under a political regime that openly legitimated such ownership and control. Thus, there was no confusion as to America's nature—it was a hypocritical democracy in service to white males whose freedom openly depended upon the oppression of blacks. It goes without saying that abolitionists argued for the end of slavery on the grounds that America could not claim to be a democracy born in the Age of Enlightenment while simultaneously trampling over blacks' human rights. They often spotlighted the shameful hypocrisy of a white democracy built on the basis of black slavery and urged their audiences to see that American institutions and citizens were actively betraying the ideals of liberty and fairness they claimed to value. Thus, slavery failed both the nation and its citizens in morally significant ways that undermined both the idea and practice of democracy.

Such shame seemed to take on a sharper and, if it can be imagined, more urgent tone after the Emancipation Proclamation had ended slavery but had failed to usher in an era of genuine black freedom. While blacks were unshackled from plantations, whites reminded them that their freedom remained dependent on whites' goodwill. But that goodwill was not forthcoming. Instead, the era of black lynching and Jim Crow filled the space formerly occupied by slavery. As Reconstruction crumbled under President Andrew Jackson's hammer blows, institutions relied less on controlling black bodies for labor and started controlling them with segregation and brutal punishment.[1] White supremacy increasingly became an unmediated relationship between common white and black Americans as well as between blacks and institutions that were de facto and often de jure agents of white power interests.

This relocation resulted in horrific acts of violence in the form of racial resentment and terror masquerading as justice. By some estimates, more than 3,400 black Americans were lynched between 1862 and 1968. To put this in perspective, the marked murder of blacks by private citizens is bracketed historically on one end by the signing of the Emancipation Proclamation and on the other end by the signing of the Civil Rights Act of 1964 and the Voting Rights Act of 1965. In other words, the years following and leading up to momentous opportunities for black freedom were filled with murderous racial terror. It's important to emphasize that the tendency to racial murder was often not without attending narratives. As Frederick Douglass and Ida B. Wells will teach us in the pages that follow, a main piece of propaganda used to justify black lynching was supposed criminality, the charge of rape of white women being especially common. The notion of black criminality was essential for white supremacists. If blacks were going to roam American streets free, then they were a threat to the lives of good, upstanding whites, and the government could not be counted on to practice exacting justice. Completely unfounded charges of crimes were offered up to turn the gears of racial vengeance within communities and institutions. Once these gears began moving, almost no person or institution could or would prevent the ensuing barbarity.

On May 15, 1916, Jesse Washington, a black teenager, was tortured and lynched in Waco, Texas. Having been charged with murder, he did get the opportunity to stand in a courtroom and in front of a jury (as opposed to many other blacks who were sentenced and executed by citizens, outside the courts). However, the surrounding circumstances could not have been more antagonistic to the idea of a fair trial. After a handful of testimonies, Washington is said to have quietly admitted to the crime of murdering Lucy Fryer, a white woman. Before the court officials could secure Washington, a posse of local residents forcibly removed him from the courthouse, placed a chain around his neck, and dragged him through town while beating and stabbing him, only to ultimately torture him for an hour before he died by hanging. As was common morbid practice, parts of Washington's body were confiscated by the bystanders, who at one point numbered fifteen thousand. His body parts were later sold as memorabilia. It wasn't enough that Washington had been decimated, his decimation had to be fetishized and profitable.

There is no question, and few would doubt, that Washington's case and the thousands like it are a great stain on America's moral record. But many Americans would also be quick to point out that lynching is a thing of the past, that we do not practice such barbaric forms of legal retribution anymore. Is that right?

In Paris, Texas, in 2008, Brandon McClelland was hit by a pickup truck driven by Shannon Finley and Ryan Crostley—two men known to be associated with white-supremacist groups—and then tethered to the back of the truck and dragged to his death. Despite the physical signs of foul play found after the truck was impounded, the two men pleaded not guilty and were subsequently released due to a lack of evidence. The miscarriage of justice in this case is all the more unsettling when we realize that one of the lynching cases that most haunted Ida B. Wells was that of Henry Smith, also of Paris, Texas, who was tortured, burned, and dismembered for an hour before being lynched in 1873. More than 130 years later, Finley and Crostley reenacted history with impunity.

Then there is the case of Eric Garner of Staten Island, New York. On July 17, 2014, Garner was confronted by Staten Island police for selling cigarettes on the street. When the police moved to confront Garner, the matter became physical, and officer Daniel Pantaleo placed Garner in a chokehold, an illegal maneuver. The incident was caught on video, and viewers can hear Garner telling Pantaleo that he can't breathe. This person sworn to protect and serve the public was thus alerted that he was actively placing an American citizen in mortal danger. Rather than acknowledge that he might be killing Garner, Pantaleo kept his grip around Garner's throat until he was dead. Thus, America was witness to a twenty-first-century lynching, and many were sure justice would prevail given the indisputable video evidence. Yet, on December 3, 2014, a grand jury failed to indict Pantaleo on any charges, allowing him, a member of law enforcement, to walk as free as Finely and Crostley.

In the pages that follow, we will revisit Ida B. Wells's pioneering efforts to use the institutions of the American media and journalism to shed light on the injustices of lynching. Her career and cause cost her, as she was exiled from Memphis, Tennessee, where she worked as an educator, owing to threats against her life. Her dedication was admirable to blacks and sympathetic whites who read her work and witnessed her activism. But first, we will engage Frederick Douglass, a thinker who began his career by using the idea of shame to fight slavery, and later took on the issue of lynching. It was fitting that Douglass realized what Wells saw so clearly—that no nation can call itself either democratic or civilized when it permits killings of and violence against its racial minorities. Not in the inner cities, not on a dark country road, and not at a presidential campaign rally.

***

> In viewing the alleged causes of the present perilous and dilapidated condition of the Federal Union, and the various plans by which it is proposed to set that Union in safety, all manly sensibility is shocked, and all human patience breaks down in disgust and indignation at the spectacle. The attitude of the Northern people in this crisis will crimson the cheeks of their children's children with shame.[2]

Frederick Douglass wrote those words in February 1861, just two months before the start of the civil war that would rock America to its foundations. They are emblematic of the way he relied on shame to respond to a racially crooked democracy. His words just a few lines later illustrate the core importance of shame: "We have been singing and shouting *free speech! free speech!* on every Northern stump during the last ten years, and yet one rebellious frown of South Carolina has muzzled the mouths of all our large cities, and filled the air with whines for compromise." For Douglass, the quickness to silence and the desire to avoid confrontation in the name of principles held dear amounted to moral cowardice of a sort that no right-thinking American should be comfortable with. The source of their discomfort should be shame. This stance was held by a man who was born a slave and fought, literally, for both his freedom and humanity. The years of compromise for Douglass had definitively concluded, and there was only hope and a wider struggle for racial justice left.

Douglass did not know his exact birthday. As he notes in his first autobiography, *Narrative of a Life*, slave masters often kept such information from their slave children. For Douglass, this was an early bit of unhappiness that in retrospect would motivate his quest to be his own person, or, as whites had long been—self-owned. As he recalled, "The white children could tell their ages. I could not tell why I ought to be deprived of the same privilege."[3] From early in his life, it would seem, Douglass had a distinct sense of inequality, namely, that white Americans were able to take comfort in their status as independent and free people and the various powers such a status comes with (like knowing when one was born). In contrast, blacks were treated as if their humanity was deeply qualified. Maybe more problematic was the basic idea that treating slaves in this way would compel them to look on their own lives in a like manner, as only being worth as much as what a white person told them it was worth. However, Douglass would never be able to live with such abject disrespect—the day would come when he would fight back for his dignity. Douglass's violent encounter with the slave master Edward Covey in his early adult years is today something of the stuff of legend. Douglass famously wrote of the encounter, "You have seen how a man was made a slave; you shall see how a slave was made a man." This line is often quoted to establish that Douglass was mortally fighting for his freedom and manhood.[4] That is, of course, true. Douglass could scarcely have written a more succinct sentence to convey the enormity of the moment.

His owner, Thomas Auld, had contracted him to work for a year for Edward Covey. Though, of course, slavery had never been kind to Douglass, he also had not experienced the level of physical abuse and disregard he would working for Covey. The initial six months were filled with beatings and whippings. It was at the six-month mark, after Covey had opened Douglass's head with a blow from a slat of wood, that Douglass seemed to decide that enough was enough. He fled through the woods back to the home of his owner, Thomas Auld, nearly bleeding to death in the process. Despite Douglass's account of his injury and the many abuses he had suffered, Auld told Douglass that he had probably deserved the beating and that he was to go back to Covey the very next day. Let us pause here for a just a moment. It is very easy to point out the direct abuses of slavery—the forced labor, physical violations, and emotional abuse. But consider the bare fact that Auld was able to and did tell Douglass, without laying a finger on him, that he was to return to the very man who had just split his skull open; and, moreover, that Douglass in fact followed his instruction. One must appreciate not only the overt and explicit vagaries of slavery but also the very system of social and moral control slavery and white supremacy made possible. Thus, when Douglass returned to Covey and fought with him for two hours—as he told it—he did more than defend himself or preempt future beatings. Douglass, rather, decided to break all the chains of both physical and mental oppression in the name of his black humanity.

Douglass returned to Covey on a Sunday, and on that day Covey seemed intent on exercising some peculiar form of Christian restraint; thus he greeted Douglass amiably and cordially. However, the rules of engagement changed on Monday; Covey cornered Douglass, intending to give him the beating he felt Douglass deserved for running away two days prior. Douglass was quite aware that if he allowed Covey to proceed, whatever bit of authority he might have asserted by fleeing would likely be lost forever. Thus, in being willing to violently confront Covey, he sought to reconstitute the terms of their mutual engagement. And he succeeded to a degree, as Covey ceased beating Douglass for the remainder of his work contract.

Douglass would be a slave for another four years, but he had succeeded in redefining for himself his status as a person with his own ideas of value. He had also succeeded to some degree in implanting this idea in Covey's mind. And it was this unexpected though desirable reconstitution that would fuel Douglass's increasing desires to be self-defining and, ultimately, self-made. Here, in the famous encounter with Covey, we find the genesis of Douglass's philosophical moorings—we each possess the vulnerability to be overtaken by oppressors, but we also possess the potential power to rewrite the rules of the relationship. For Douglass, this meant a direct physical confrontation while a slave. It is all the more remarkable, then, that Douglass went on to spend his life speaking and thereby teaching about the experiences of slaves in order to do for them what he had managed to do for himself: reconstitute the idea of black humanity in the minds of white Americans. He did this primarily by leveraging the idea and ideals of American democracy to call out the hypocrisy, thus the shameworthiness, of racial oppression.[5]

It would be fourteen years after fleeing aboard a northern-bound train toward freedom in 1838, that Douglass would deliver his landmark address, "What, to the Slave, Is the Fourth of July?" Although it was only one of many dozens of addresses Douglass delivered in his lengthy career, it is not only his best known but arguably provides a rhetorical and philosophical key for almost all his other writings. This is not to say Douglass was in the business of merely repackaging the same speeches. Rather, as with all great intellectuals, Douglass had an angle on understanding the world and a way of conceptualizing the art of persuasion that ran like DNA through his great corpus. While a great many things could be said about his presentation—indeed, a discussion of it could span an entire chapter if not a book—I want to emphasize three aspects or strategies that served Douglass well in his writings.

The first, essential strategy of "What, to the Slave, Is the Fourth of July?" is maybe the most remarked upon but is nonetheless crucial. On July 5, 1852, Douglass presented comments regarding the Independence Day holiday. Speaking to a predominantly white audience at Corinthian Hall in Rochester, New York, Douglass faced a choice—he could either present a standard commemoration of the day, or, having access to a white audience, he could press them on the meaning of the holiday. Douglass chose the latter. Indeed, he wasted no time making his audience aware that he and they did not stand in the hall as equals, that he and they did not come to occupy that hall from the same place in America. He also explained how these essential forms of inequality and difference born of oppression placed them on different sides of the holiday. Thus, Douglass consistently referred to the Fourth of July holiday and the nation it cele-brates as belonging to his audience, not to him. For example, reflecting on the genesis of the holiday, Douglass remarked, "The freedom gained is yours; and you, therefore, may prop-erly celebrate this anniversary. The Fourth of July is the first great fact in your nation's history[.]"[6]

Douglass's use of the pronoun "your" indicates a distinc-tion between him and his audience, but the strategy wouldn't have been worth much if that had been all Douglass was up to. Who in the room could reasonably have believed that even though Douglass was now a free man, he and his audience would naturally share the same perspective? No, Douglass meant more. Indeed, in drawing the distinction between himself and his audience he asserted the authority of moral insight that he gained as a former slave.[7] Douglass used this authority to highlight that the distinction between him and his audience was not only intrinsically bad but explainable by hypocrisy and moral laziness. In this regard, he urged his audience to what we might call *moral realignment*—the call for Americans to act consistently from the values and principles of democratic freedom. As simple as it may seem to us today, Douglass and others of his time felt the quarrel wasn't with the idea of America or with democracy. Quite the opposite. He felt these ideas could be leveraged to bring to life the ideal of America encoded in the Constitution and in the very act of American revolution the holiday signified.

This leads to his third strategy—to initiate in the moral imagination of his audience members the idea of *national redemption through civic virtue*. Consider this extended passage:

> By an act of the American congress, not yet two years old, slavery has been nationalized in its most horrible and revolting form. . . . The power to hold, hunt, and sell men, women, and children as slaves remains no longer a mere state institution but is now an institution of the whole United States. The power is coextensive with the star-spangled banner. . . . Your lawmakers have commanded all good citizens to engage in this hellish sport.[8]

Here, Douglass asked his audience to consider the odious Fugitive Slave Act, which Congress had passed in 1850 to allow average citizens to capture slaves who fled their masters. The idea was that Americans could and should help slave owners reclaim their property. The offensiveness of the law is not hard to estimate. What Douglass did think the average listener in his audience might fail to appreciate, however, was the relationship between the legitimacy Congress bestowed on such an offensive action by inscribing it into the law of the land and in making the everyday American complicit in and obligated to oppress blacks, even if they did not own slaves themselves. It must have struck Douglass and the abolitionists as shocking that the branch of government most closely associated with the will of the people was itself shaping that will by effectively democratizing the control and restraint of black bodies and lives.

Together, Douglass's distinctions between moral perspectives, desire for moral realignment, and urging for national redemption through civic virtue represent his main project, a democratic reimagining. Which is to say, it was necessary for Douglass that July day in 1852, and every other time he took the podium, that his audience members be able to shed the practices of the America they knew in order to envision an America marked by greater consistency with its professed ethical principles. This was the trick: the resources for doing so were the very principles that were already in play in our polity. In a way, Douglass felt that the obstacles to moral improvement were substantial, since Americans had developed and were institutionally motivated to develop racially offensive habits. On the other side of the problem, his grounds for hope consisted in the notion that America didn't need a new founding. It needed, rather, a new and genuine acknowledgment of the attitudes, dispositions, and policies that the founding committed the everyday American to uphold.

What then, if anything, could be decisive in shifting America to act more in accord with the principles upon which it was founded? Despite his high-minded ideals and what must have seemed to him in the quiet of his own mind lofty goals to redeem what many other blacks judged to be an irredeemable nation, Douglass was not naïve. Grounded assessment and keen insight urged Douglass to tackle the problem from both angles. On the one hand, the institutions that sanctioned slavery needed to be brought to heel. On the other, better policies, while certainly helpful in reshaping citizens' habits, would not be sufficient if it turned out that everyday white Americans remained morally ignorant of and cold toward blacks' claim that their lives mattered. Let us address the first aspect. What can be said of Douglass's commentary on institutions?

We should be mindful that at the time of Douglass's writing and activism, the idea of American institutions had not taken on the more sprawling nature it possesses today. The nation was still young, and the Constitution barely eighty years old. The Constitution, then, remained one of the most visible institutions of the nation. Moreover, it was rightly considered the document that gave America its unique democratic character. It is not surprising that advocates of slavery as well as abolitionists turned to the document for legal and moral support.

From Douglass's perspective, reading the Constitution as a document in support of slavery rested on at least two sorts of philosophical sloppiness. The first was that those on the side of slavery imputed to the founding document a stance in favor of slavery because the government itself supported slavery. On Douglass's view, this simply begged the question of whether the government was in fact acting legitimately and faithfully to its founding laws and precepts: "The Constitution may be right, the Government wrong. If the Government has been governed by mean, sordid, and wicked passions, it does not follow that that the Constitution is mean, sordid, and wicked."⁹ This move by Douglass is deeply important. If the strategy to read the founding document through the immoral practices of the government went unchecked, then blacks would find themselves susceptible to a most tragic conservatism, since, indeed, the wickedness of slave holders would be taken as part and parcel with American democracy. It would be a conservatism that honored not just the past but a crooked past that displayed the worst aspects of human society.

The second strategy Douglass responded to was one holding that even if explicit textual support for slavery was not to be found in the Constitution, then its support could be found in the support of the attitudes and intentions of the founders. This strategy was remarkably sly since it was in fact true that early luminaries, including Thomas Jefferson and George Washington, owned slaves. Thus, if they had owned slaves *and* had founded the nation, they must have envisioned America as a slaveholding nation. But Douglass's response was more astute than sly, and thus on firmer ground. He noted two features of the deliberations that had informed the formation of the Constitution. First, the deliberations were held behind closed doors with the goal of generating a document that could stand on its own for all of America's future years, rather than be identified with the historically contingent beliefs of a group of men who would be gone long before the nation truly reached maturity. Second, even if the debates could be thought of as resources for interpreting the Constitution, it did not seem it was the founders' intention that the debates be used thusly. As Douglass rightly noted, "[T]the debates in the convention that framed the Constitution, and by means of which a pro-slavery interpretation is now attempted . . . were not published till more than a quarter of a century after [its adoption]."[10]

For Douglass, to act in line with the basic principles of equality and fairness, institutions faced a bar higher than just considering whether laws were in place to treat blacks appropriately. Instead, they needed to consider whether the right laws were in place to educate and habituate the citizens over which they held sway. This is why Douglass remained steadfast in his reading of the Constitution as taking a position for reform over revolution. His position, as in that of his Fourth of July address, was to hold the ideal of American institutions as both unrealized and as ideals worth fighting to realize. However, he was concerned elsewhere that if American institutions failed to conform to the ideals they represented, they themselves would engender in the polity unfortunate dispositions. More than the already morally awful desire to own and physically suppress black people encouraged by policies like the Fugitive Slave Law, Douglass was also concerned about the effects of such institutions on blacks themselves: "Can the colored man be expected to entertain for such a government any feelings but those of intense hatred? Or can he be expected to do other than to seize the first moment which shall promise him success to gratify his vengeance?"[11]

A recurring theme throughout this book, and, indeed, one that continues to play a role in blacks' lives as we continue to grapple with what it means to be both American citizens and also, in many senses, endangered despite our legal status, is how it is blacks should think of forgiveness and forbearance toward American institutions and whites. I have already remarked on the ways in which Douglass sought to activate within whites a sense of shame to enliven their moral imagination and sense of civic obligation. However, Douglass sought to live by his own strategies. His letters to Captain Thomas Auld, his owner before he had, in his words, become a man, are poignantly exemplary of this aspiration.

The first of two letters I want to consider was written in 1848, ten years after Douglass had run away from Auld. Indeed, the tone of Douglass's letter to Auld was celebratory, as if marking an anniversary. What did he hope to gain by writing Auld, who no longer held power over him? Douglass invited, as he noted in the letter, a renewed bounty on his head by writing to Auld in the public newspaper *The Liberator*. But maybe the question about Douglass's purpose is misguided in one or more ways. Maybe the point wasn't that Auld still had power but that those like Auld who perpetuated slavery had power they ought not to have. Or, maybe Auld himself did have power over Douglass, but not in all the problematic ways we might assume. It could be that the value and texture of Douglass's freedom and his initiatives as a free man were inextricably linked to his time with Auld. I think both the above are true.

Douglass did not hesitate to provide a bit of philosophical insight into the problem of identity under slavery, and, in this way, his missive to Auld was an instrument for moving his audience to reflect on a much broader set of concerns. Douglass stated that his sense of self became a problem after he overheard older slaves saying that there were black persons in the world who were not forced to serve whites, and that there was a place called Africa from which people like him came and where they were free. Douglass rightly concluded that his station in life was therefore unnatural. It took only this realization for Douglass to decide he would run away. He imagined, of course, that despite the inherent rightness of wanting to be free, he would need to justify seizing his freedom over the investments whites had made in the structures of power that had forced blacks into servitude. Douglass articulated it this way: "We are distinct persons, and are each equally provided with faculties necessary to our individual existence. In leaving you, I took nothing but what belonged to me, and in no way lessened your means for obtaining an honest living."[12] This way of putting the problem applied categorically between any two persons defined by relations of ownership and being owned, and thus served as a kind of philosophical response to the unethical nature of slaveholding.

But writing in public, Douglass once again put shame to use. He chronicled the intimacy of the abuses he had suffered as Auld's slave for his readers. And he also damningly catalogued the many family members he believed Auld still owned, including a grandmother who was old and ailing at the time of Douglass's escape ten years earlier, and who ought to have been set free by Auld out of mercy.[13] But Douglass did more than list complaints. He connected the moral gravity of his complaints to the possibility for moral responsibility. He knew that he couldn't simply indict Auld, or any slaveholder. He had to do the hard work of inviting Auld to take up a position of opprobrium against himself—hence, shame. Douglass wrote, "The responsibility which you have assumed in this regard is truly awful—and how you could stagger under it these many years is truly marvellous. Your mind must have become darkened, your heart hardened, your conscience seared and petrified, or you would have long since thrown off the accursed load and sought relief at the hands of a sin-forgiving God."[14] Though these lines surely have the tone of a straightforward indictment, coming to that conclusion misses a crucial feature. In that statement, Douglass neither insulted Auld nor made assertions about the kind of person Auld was. Rather, he invited Auld to take stock of his own character by speculating as to what must have happened to Auld over the years. In this way, Douglass wanted Auld to ask himself the question: how could one person do such things to another person? While this is philosophically interesting, we should ask the practical question: does shame ever work?

One year later, Douglass once again took to the pages of *The Liberator*, this time to celebrate the eleventh anniversary of his freedom, but now he had a very different message for Auld—one of congratulation. Douglass learned that Auld had set his slaves, thus Douglass's family, free, save for the ailing grandmother who was deemed too old to be able to care for herself. She was freed but remained in Auld's care. There are many remarkable aspects to Douglass's second letter to Auld. It stands as a testament to the fact that though one who had suffered the depredations Douglass had might thus be justified in one's indignation, he might nevertheless make a moral contribution to the world by instead pursuing a project of moral co-development and progress. Let me highlight just one aspect that seems to bring together the potential for moral argument and the possibility for genuine civic uptake.

Douglass congratulated Auld. But this congratulation was not laden with resentment or irony. Rather, it was genuine for Douglass. Others, including James Baldwin, whom we will meet in a later chapter, would powerfully argue that in many ways whites were victims of their own systems of power, as Douglass did: "Born and brought up in the presence and under the influence of a system which at once strikes at the very foundation of morals . . . it is almost impossible that one so environed can greatly grow in virtuous rectitude." Yet Auld proved for Douglass that "the heart of the slaveholder is still within reach of the truth"—and Douglass's work in preceding years, including his previous letter, had made a public civic contribution to the uses of the truth. Which is to say, the many addresses in which Douglass compelled whites to take account of their actions and attitudes in comparison to the values they claimed to uphold seemed to have had the desired impact on no less than his former owner.[15]

Despite the clearly problematic attitudes that continued to make slavery and racism a treacherous problem for America, Douglass was on the front lines in addressing a public that required and needed moral re-education. To be clear, few people needed to be informed about what was wrong with slavery. Douglass maintained throughout his career that the moral point against slavery was clear and plain. The main thing the American public needed was a way of being able to connect ideas of rightness and wrongness to treatment of blacks, a class of persons whose humanity was constantly questioned, threatened, and denied. Despite Douglass's considerable successes in the abstract in being able to build a career as a very public and vocal abolitionist, darker days were coming. It would surely be cavalier to somehow suggest that the years leading up to, during, and immediately following the Civil War were somehow enlightened just because the issue of slavery was front and center and then later decided in favor of abolition. America remained trenchantly racist and hostile to blacks throughout. However, under the system of slavery, there was very little confusion as to blacks' wretched position in America, and masters did not seek to hide their abuse of slaves. Yes, this was awful, but it was also transparent. What came after the collapse of Reconstruction would be a new kind of systematic evil that resulted in horrors no democracy ought to host.

> If the American conscience were only half alive, if the American church and clergy were only half Christianized[,] if American moral sensibility were not hardened by persistent infliction of outrage and crime against colored people, a scream of horror, shame, and indignation would rise to Heaven wherever your pamphlet shall be read.[16]

The age of Jim Crow lynching became the issue of the day for civil rights activists as Douglass's career was coming to a close. His above words comprised the preface for Ida B. Wells's important and maybe longest writing on American lynching. Douglass had a spent a lifetime writing and speaking against slavery and shaming a nation to set blacks free. At the close of the nineteenth century and after the collapse of Reconstruction, wherein blacks were denied the promised resources to set them on a new and more prosperous path in America, lynching took the place of slavery as the momentous sin. It was Ida B. Wells's turn to bring shame to the American people.

Ida B. Wells was sitting at a meeting in Jersey City, New Jersey, with Thomas T. Fortune, founding editor of the black publication *New York Age*, when he told her she couldn't go back home to Memphis, Tennessee. Having been born into slavery, as Wells had been, and having made a name for himself in journalism, as Wells had recently begun to do, he understood the implications of the events unfolding in her hometown. Fortune showed her the copy of the *New York Sun* he was carrying, which had run a story describing how the offices of Wells's own publication, *Free Speech*, had been destroyed by a mob. The mob's reason? Wells had written a characteristically forceful and damning editorial on the lynching of three local black men. Aggrieved and offended local whites made it clear that if she returned home she would be next—she would become a victim of the murderous vigilante justice she had dared to expose to a nation.

The three victims—Thomas Moss, Calvin McDowell, and Henry Stewart—were the proprietors of a grocery store in a dominantly black suburb. Their establishment was situated directly across the street from the only other grocery store in town, which happened to be white-owned. The trouble began when some white and black boys got into a scuffle over a game of marbles, a fight the black boys won. The situation escalated when the "father of the white boys whipped the victorious colored boy, whose father and friends pitched in to avenge the grown white man's flogging of a colored boy."[17] Needless to say, in 1892, no such justified retaliation on the part of blacks would be tolerated by whites. Some days later, after a failed armed retribution by whites at the site of the grocery store, more than one hundred black men were removed from their homes and put in holding cells with the participation of local officials. Here, whites came to view them and picked out the men who had dared to defend themselves and their children. Moss, McDowell, and Stewart were removed and put in a railroad carriage, taken a mile outside of city limits, and riddled with shotgun blasts.

Lynching was not a new phenomenon in America, nor had it been used as a gruesome form of civic vengeance on blacks exclusively. But, in the years following the signing of the Emancipation Proclamation and the collapse of Reconstruction, real white lawlessness rose to a pitch that exceeded the fabricated stories of black lawlessness. The idea of the black superpredator, given this specific name by political scientist and criminologist John DiLulio in 1995, predates our recent racial political troubles by more than a century. It was fostered with narratives that freed blacks were a danger to upstanding whites, especially white women.[18] In the case of the Curve Lynching, as Wells referred to it, the white press justified the arrest of the many scores of black men by telling the white public a tale of black men firing on law-upholding white police officers who were supposedly searching for a criminal. Not only was the story a complete fiction, but it also omitted the preceding circumstances of blacks having to defend themselves from a vengeance they hadn't deserved in the first place. Thus, Wells, in writing on the Curve Lynching and many others, was a leader among those on the front lines of a predicament blacks and #BlackLivesMatter activists continue to face today—resisting narratives of deviance that justify and exculpate murderous violations of blacks' civil rights.

If shame is the appropriate moral response to one's failing to be consistent with one's own ideals and professed principles, then it will be true that certain vices call for shame. Maybe the most consonant vice is hypocrisy. Though hypocrisy is commonly thought of as when a person believes or says one thing but then proceeds to act in ways contrary to the belief or statement, there is one particular feature of hypocrisy that is crucial for contextualizing Wells's fight against lynching—the violation of reliable expectations between hope and justice.

One of the facts of American life that was most precious and fragile in the aftermath of the signing of the Emancipation Proclamation was blacks' freedom. As we saw, Douglass spent his public career speaking against slavery on the basic but powerful grounds that the notion of owning humans in America was distinctly at odds with the very idea and justification for the American nation—that every person is born free with certain inalienable rights. America, then, was founded as a nation whose government would enshrine this basic assertion without contesting its validity—it was simply accepted that persons were born free and were meant to be treated equally. Of course, these ideals were violated in any number of ways, not least by the slaughter and displacement of Native Americans across North America. But blacks experienced this slippage between laudable values and morally offensive practices in a different, though no less acute, way. Rather than being displaced, they were held close to white society precisely so that they could be oppressed and used in every manner imaginable. The Emancipation Proclamation disrupted the standard structure of that relationship by decoupling black labor and bodies from lands and enterprises owned by whites. When blacks had been bound to the land, other forms of repression were elementary. So it was a simple matter to restrict a slave's movement during work hours by, for example, posting overseers on plantations. But un-reconstructed whites questioned how to maintain the degree of control they had once exerted when blacks gained greater mobility and liberty. The answer few spoke of but that was enacted more than three thousand times in the following century was to kill any black person whites felt constituted a threat to their authority. The average white citizen became the overseer, thereby extending the scope of oppression and rendering null the promise of emancipation. The age of lynching, then, stood as a critical and dangerous challenge to the bridge Douglass had fought so hard to build between hope and democracy, for that bridge was built on the assumption that formal liberty would dissolve the will of supremacists. Supremacists responded with murderous recalcitrance, signaling that blacks' liberty would be met with shows of force that worked either in conjunction with or outside the bounds of the law. Wells inherited the corruption of post-Emancipation society and politics and put the press to work to renew the call to shame.

Wells pressed her case on two fronts. On the one hand, the law was being disregarded in fundamental ways that undercut blacks' ability to see local and national government as protecting their freedom or ensuring fairness—"We have reached the unprecedented low level; the criminal depravity of substituting the mob for the court and jury, of giving up the jail keys to the mob whenever they are demanded."[19] For Wells, the ability of extrajudicial racist mobs to intervene in the justice system before a suspect ever stepped foot in a court, or to remove suspects from jails before a sentence could be served represented a deep corruption of the democratic ethos. In such instances the rule of law that is meant to bind citizens to each other by way of the social contract became what she often referred to as the "unwritten law" of "lynch law." It amounted to little more than the culmination of racial resentment and hatred as feigned sincerity in the pursuit of justice. "Lynch law" represented the absolute worst vices of white supremacy, at its most fervent, with none of the virtues of democratic equality. Whites simply decided to take possession of the law—something meant to belong to the people—and use it for their own interests.

But in many ways, this is very much the dynamic Wells was fighting, for who were "the people" of the United States? Douglass, her public predecessor, spent his career making the case to expand the very notion of "the people" to include black Americans. Indeed, this was the singular power of his address, "What, To the Slave, Is the Fourth of July?" The main obstacle standing in the way of that expansion was the full legal emancipation of slaves and the passage of laws that institutionalized racial equality. Not that Douglass was so naïve as to think that laws could do all the work—if so, his reliance on the idea of shame would be nonsensical. Nonetheless, the first bar to be cleared was the expansion of who counted as a real and legitimate American. Blacks had paid their dues and had been dragged to the land of liberal democracy, thus they were owed full inclusion as both victims and as humans whose interests and well-being mattered.

In the aftermath of the Emancipation Proclamation, however, Wells faced a tricky problem. The idea of the people had supposedly been expanded in favor of blacks' inclusion, but the actions of un-reconstructed whites cut right across the bow of legal equality. It didn't help that the laws were often complicit in undoing the work of emancipation, such as Jim Crow laws that sanctioned segregation. The fight against slavery had been concluded in a legal manner; yet, it was also true that the question of blacks' acceptance and inclusion into civic society had failed to be settled in anything remotely resembling a satisfactory manner. The institutional slavery that had enshrined the very idea of black oppression may have been vanquished, but not so the civic hatred and rejection that filled the space slavery had occupied. Civil society embraced its inheritance of racial supremacy and played out its hatred in the form of lynching, a form of extrajudicial justice that the legal system either seemed unwilling to interfere with or, quite often, was openly complicit in aiding. The significance of Wells's work, then, was that her "efforts against lynching shed light on the ways in which black bodies became the site of a shifting contest over civil rights and physical integrity, over human dignity and social power."[20] This, then, highlighted the relationship between politics, race, and everyday democratic life.

In a July 1893 essay, Wells noted that more than fifty blacks had been lynched since the beginning of that year. Of these, "One man was under the protection of the governor of South Carolina, and he gave him up to the mob that promptly lynched him. A state senator was prominently mentioned in connection with the lynching. No concealment was attempted."[21] To our contemporary ears, though we may have finally come to accept the unreliability of police integrity, the participation of a senator and state governor in a black murder strikes us as absurd. Yet, the very fact that, as Wells put it, no concealment was made itself shows just how deeply entrenched white supremacy was not only in the hearts of the average American but also in the practices of political elites.

It stands to reason, then, that in a democracy, the key would be voting to remove officials who fail to uphold the most basic tenets of post-slavery liberal democracy. It was for this reason Wells thought that wide enfranchisement would bring an end to lynching. Of course, the idea of democratic responsiveness is as basic as the idea of political representation is old. Wells observed, in 1910, "The Negro has been given separate and inferior schools, because he has no ballot. He therefore cannot protest against such legislation by choosing other lawmakers, or retiring to private life those who legislate against his interests."[22] In the preceding ten years, Southern states had systematically instituted various measures to suppress black voting, such as poll taxes and literacy tests. The suppression of the franchise translated directly into the complete absence of political influence. And, without political influence, blacks were deprived the means to effect the necessary political change for their safety and liberties under the law.

But this raised the issue as to whether lynch law was fundamental to our society. Just as Douglass had argued that the Constitution offered no protections for slavery, so Wells argued with respect to the deep asymmetry of political and social power that facilitated lynching, "Although the Constitution specially says, no state shall do so, they *do* deprive persons of life, liberty and property without due process of law, and *do* deny equal protection of the laws to persons of Negro descent" (422). Wells clearly intended to highlight a rupture between what states are obligated to do and what they in fact do, but her invocation of the Constitution was especially significant. Wells could just have easily said that national law prohibited the actions states permitted within their borders or undertook directly with respect to the suppression of black rights and well-being. Instead, she invoked the Constitution, a document whose symbolism extends beyond the laws it prescribes and proscribes. This document founded the United States as a nation that valued its liberty. It did so on the grounds that the absence of representation in the British Crown put the autonomy of its political subjects, guaranteed by the idea of natural rights, in jeopardy. The Constitution's signature value is that it centers the entire being of the nation on the very ideas of equal liberty and the primacy of the law. Otherwise, the very project of democratic living would be forfeit. If revolutionaries had not been fighting for the law of individual liberty, the fight against the English crown would have been a hypocritical pretext for war, simpliciter. Wells's gamble in invoking the Constitution was that no Americans were willing to mortgage the ideals of American democracy for mere racial pride, so foundational markers like that hallowed document were used to remind Americans of essential features of a proper democratic life. Not that this was noticeably successful.

Wells pushed her arguments through and across many analytic avenues. Her multifaceted strategies indicate the tight and tragic relationship between the racist heart of America at a visceral personal level and institutions at an impersonal but no less visceral level. As a journalist, the second front Wells pressed her case against, she clearly believed in the power of the press to move the American people, but there were deep issues here also. Wells excoriated the press—the institution thought so intrinsic to democracy and the balance of power on the side of the people—because it was failing its duty to report the news.[23] As Wells charged, "The American press, with few exceptions, either by [bad] editorials or silence, has encouraged mobs, and is responsible for the increasing wave of lawlessness which is sweeping over the States."[24] Wells saw this as a critical failing. She had given up her home and way of life in the name of freedom of speech to report on and expose the problem of lynching. Though it is of course without doubt that this was done in service to social justice, Wells's sacrifice additionally undergirded her view that institutions like the press modeled the best aspirations of democracy since freedom of speech equalized the distribution of power to some degree. The modernization of print media offered promising new opportunities to spread the truth of racial terrorism, but, as Jacqueline Goldsby has pointed out, its success as a mass media also imposed serious obstacles; newspapers placed markets above truth. This left Wells to navigate a malleable but problematic media landscape: "This, after all, was why she went to such lengths to publish pamphlets. Each booklet invited readers to join an alternative economy that valued knowledge not as a market commodity but as a moral commitment to examine how newspapers defined what mattered as history."[25] Of course, if the press shaped itself to the vested interests of white supremacists then the value of the ideal of free speech was greatly reduced. What good is a press that fails to report the facts, at best, or spread falsehoods, at worst?

For these reasons, Wells felt that blacks in Southern journalism had a special role in the fight for racial justice and the soul of American democracy. Indeed, in "The Requirements of Southern Journalism," Wells suggested at least three specific functions a robust Southern press should strive to fulfill. The first of these was to educate blacks, since many blacks had not received much formal education. The press in these instances could help instruct blacks in, as Wells put it, "the science of civil government."[26] Second, Wells held that through the dissemination of facts true to the black experience and its educative effects, a robust press could help secure for blacks both a stronger sense of solidarity, or what the political scientist Michael Dawson has influentially identified as "linked fate," and a stronger sense of one's own liberties.[27] Third, and very importantly, the black Southern press had on Wells's view a unique obligation to make a contribution to changing the sentiment of Americans at large. The white-controlled press had by and large complied with the mandates of white supremacy and Jim Crow thinking by regurgitating the notion that blacks were a threat to white well-being, especially that of white women, and that most cases of lynching had been necessary or could be justified on the grounds of protecting the honor of white women from sexual assault and the integrity of white society at large from the looming threat of black criminality more generally. Such narratives did little else than reinforce the image of blacks as uncivilized and bestial, unthinking creatures ruled by lust rather than by rationality, and thus dangerous and deserving of the mob justice they often met.

Wells would not and could not stand for these misrepresentations of blacks. She bore witness to a nation that had set blacks free from plantations only to become enslaved by the specter of death meted out by resentfully racist mobs. Slavery, in comparison, must have seemed easier to fight against—it was a large economic institution wherein one could easily quantify the profits slave labor enabled, as one could count the bales of cotton slaves manufactured and the black bodies that made American industry thrive. With the collapse of slavery, the oversight of blacks devolved into a treacherous practice of accuse first, kill second, and ask questions later, if ever. So the problem was simple: how could blacks possibly do anything with the freedom they had acquired from the plantation if their everyday lives failed to mirror the hope and promise of democracy—the protection from arbitrary uses of power that deny one the pursuit of happiness?

On June 2, 2016, Jasmine Richards, founder of the Pasadena, California chapter of Black Lives Matter, was convicted of "felony lynching" and sentenced to ninety days in prison and three years' probation. The case sets a dangerous precedent, and its legal aspects are crucial to understanding its significance.

Richards was arrested in September 2015 following an incident two days earlier in which a woman was accused by a local restaurant owner of not paying her bill and assaulting the owner and employees. At a park across the street from the restaurant, Black Lives Matter activists happened to be protesting unjustified arrests and excessive police force. After observing the arrival of the police and their physical treatment of the woman at the restaurant, the activists, led by Richards, attempted to remove the woman from police custody.

Richards was charged and convicted under California Penal Code 405a, the state's so-called lynching law, which

creates a special category of offense for "a person who par-
ticipates in the taking by means of a riot of another person
from the lawful custody of a peace officer." Richards did in
fact interfere with a police action on the part of a person
who might have committed a crime, and other protesters
apparently verbally supported her. So the charge appears
to make sense. Why, then, should her arrest and conviction trouble us? The essential answer is that activists and
intellectuals such as Wells spent a lifetime moving the
American government and its people to see lynching as
an awful tragedy visited upon blacks simply because they
are black. Close to one hundred years later, the success
achieved by Wells and later activists has been turned back
on an activist whose central mandate has been to publicly,
politically affirm the very thing Wells had—that black lives
matter.

However, Richards's case moves beyond irony. Just two
months before her arrest, California governor Jerry Brown
signed legislation introduced by state senator Holly Mitchell
that cut the word "lynching" from the penal code. The bill
was introduced after Maile Hampton, another Black Lives
Matter protester, was charged for the same offense, though a
deputy district attorney wound up downgrading the charges
to misdemeanor interference with an officer. In a statement
about the legislation to revise the language of the law, Mitchell
explained that " 'lynching' has such a painful history for African
Americans that the law should only use it for what it is—
murder by mob."

Some have applauded the revision of the penal code. But
removing the word has two worrying repercussions. For one
thing, the law has lost its historical power to call an actual
lynching what it is—a crime of hate most often motivated

by race. But there is another concern. As the legal scholar, Richard H. McAdams has argued, the law has expressive power. It coordinates information, and it establishes norms and values that citizens take up. In the case of the California penal code, the removal of "lynching" introduces an important and concerning irony.[28] Lynch law was designed to prevent or respond to interference with law enforcement, since often, that interference was expedited with murderous intent. As University of Southern California law professor Jody Armour said, "The precise evil that the lawmakers designed the law to punish and prevent was lynching, not just the taking of a person from police custody, but in order to murder them."[29] However, Richards did not intervene to harm the woman under arrest, as a lynch mob might have, but to protect her. The state has thus repurposed a law that powerfully protected blacks from mob violence for its own interests: blacks themselves can now be easily accused of lynching, if not now in explicit name then in legal formality. In other words, the expressive power of the revised law is that those fighting for social justice are now an equivalent sort of threat to those who once removed blacks from police custody for the purposes of murdering them. The revised law seeks to place an impenetrable wall between those genuinely seeking to disrupt the abuse of state power; and, with respect to race, this generates the ironic result that blacks, who often are at the receiving end of state abuse, run the risk of being accused of the very crime they suffered for more than a century, often with the complicity of the state. This results in what strikes many of those who sympathize with Black Lives Matter—both as a movement and as a principle—as a perverse sort of irony. Richards's conviction and harsh sentencing makes it seem that mob rule—the removal of blacks from civic life—has been institutionalized by the state to suppress organized resistance of unjust state power.

The ironic inversion of lynch law, the punching of a black man at a presidential rally, and the continued killing of black Americans by police are evidence that Douglass's and Wells's call for national shame is not yet outdated. At the turn of the century, Douglass roused a nation to reflect on the hypocrisy of celebrating national independence in a country that practiced slavery; Ida B. Wells called on the national conscience to reject mob rule and violence. Both thinkers challenged Americans to think more clearly and consistently about the principles on which their citizenship was founded and the ways those principles were violated when blacks demanded equality. Actions of contemporary activists have injected a historical understanding of how the law and the broader civic ethos continue to work against the interests of blacks. They also, following Douglass's lead, have invoked the principles of American democracy to call upon citizens to account for the quality and content of their civic and moral convictions. They have presented to us, as a society, a picture of a people unsustainably divided by the content of our distinct perceptions. They have sought to alert us that the longer we can reasonably say that "this is your freedom and not ours," the greater the peril our polity faces of moving beyond redemption.

CULTURAL CONTROL

AGAINST SOCIAL CONTROL

The Radical Possibilities of the Harlem Renaissance

> *Listen, kids who die—*
> *Maybe, now, there will be no monument for you*
> *Except in our hearts.*
> *Maybe your bodies'll be lost in a swamp,*
> *Or in a prison grave, or the potter's field,*
> *Or the rivers where you're drowned like Liebknecht,*
> *But the day will come—*
> —LANGSTON HUGHES, *"Kids Who Die"*

"WE GONNA BE ALRIGHT!" THESE four words were chanted by Black Lives Matters protesters on an overcast day late in July 2015 as they faced down an imposing Cleveland, Ohio police force. The chant seemed straightforward bravado, almost as if to signal to the police lined up against them that their wills were indomitable. That may be part of the story but isn't the whole story.

Just a few weeks earlier, on June 28, rising hip-hop star and urban wordsmith Kendrick Lamar performed the song those four words were drawn from—"Alright"—at the BET music awards. One of the many potent tracks from his critically acclaimed and provocatively titled second major studio release, *To Pimp a Butterfly*, the song presents a kaleidoscope of black struggles, some internal to the community but, crucially, all happening against a certain background—police brutality. So, the staging for Lamar's performance was important. His backdrop was the least controversial symbol one can use in a performance for the American public—a large, digital replica of the American flag blowing in the wind. Even the most jaded of us would have a hard time resisting the image's patriotic motivational power. The tenor of the performance was meant to be tense, however—not celebratory. The all-American imagery of hope and goodness serves as the mere background for another image that we've come to accept as all-American but maybe in a more tragic sense: a cop car. But that was not all there was to the staging. If the cop car had just been sitting on stage, the tension between it and the flag would have been invisible to all but those most sensitive to the many police-perpetrated deaths that have plagued the black community. No, Lamar wanted his audience to appreciate his performance not as hip-hop braggadocio but as *rebellion*. The cop car on stage was demolished as if bombed out, and he, powerfully and defiantly, stood on top of it, performing the song that Black Lives Matter protesters would draw on weeks later. They insisted they would be all right in the face of the police, because Lamar said it on top of a demolished police car—a contemporary symbol of state oppression that had been reappropriated as a sign of defiance and empowerment, first by a musician, then by grassroots organizers and protesters who refused to be intimidated.

In foregrounding the demolished car Lamar shifted the frame of reference for the waving American flag from a symbol of hope and goodness to one of hypocrisy and threat. By standing on top of the demolished car, he meant to invoke in his audience's imagination a day when justice would be triumphant. That the car is demolished suggests maybe justice would come by violent means. Or, maybe, the imagery was meant to be more sophisticated and provocative—that continued black resistance to being defined as deviant and worthless would ultimately be the downfall of institutional corruption and a cause for national shame. Lamar was the citizen as artist *and* radical. Lamar was entering into conversation with a rich, but now less prominent, black American era that conceived art as both political and radical: the Harlem Renaissance. Knowingly or not, he helped mobilize political activists with the power of art; he insisted that black lives matter on stage, while protesters, with renewed vigor, insisted on it in the streets. Art was the conduit for both politics and emotion.

To be sure, the Harlem Renaissance was not the first time art had been used for more assertive political means. It wasn't even the first time art had been used this way by blacks. Slave songs moaned and chanted in the fields were the earliest forms of black radical art. However, what made the Renaissance distinctive and urgent is that for the first time in black history, it seemed to represent something of a collective epoch, an insurgent era, marked by the promise of a reinvigorated effort to redefine black creative life and to reassert black civic presence. The Renaissance was a period with many agents for social change. Novelists, poets, dramatists, and visual artists from across the range of black experiences sought to contribute to making black political art not only relevant but influential. In what follows I am particularly interested in the preoccupation some

Renaissance creators had with the idea of art as a mirror to the ways of life of common black folk in America. Langston Hughes and Zora Neale Hurston were especially guided by the democratic ethos of black art serving as a model for American life.

It is interesting, then, to note that "the Harlem Renaissance," while the most enduring and romantic name for the era, was not its first name. Rather, it was coined initially as the New Negro Movement, a moment of uplift and self-definition meant to stand in stark contrast with the surrounding conditions of racial oppression, lynching, and segregation—the conditions of black life not mattering.[1]

People can migrate in many ways. Of course, there is physical migration—a mass transfusion or dispersal of human bodies from one or many other geographical locations. A variety of factors can cause migrations. Sometimes the causes are economic, such as the hope for better job prospects. Sometimes people migrate to escape social circumstances such as marginalization and hostile treatment by other social groups. Other times, reasons can be political—a hope for better chances at self-determination and participation, or, at least, civic visibility. In the case of black Americans at the beginning of the twentieth century, the reason for migration turned out to be a combination of all three. World War I had put the might of American industry into motion, thus there was an unprecedented thirst for paid labor regardless of race. This was the pulling force, while conditions of social oppression, racial violence, and political suppression in the South offered the push for blacks to move northward and westward in the 1910s and 1920s—the Great Migration, wherein an estimated 1.6 million black Americans decided it was time to build their dreams and visions of the future in other parts of America.

A people can move physically but can also shift spiritually. A kind of collective sense of possibility and renewal can prompt them to seek new forms of expression, interpret the old with fresh insight, or build the new out of respect for the old ways without missing the chance for novelty and cultural adventure. Such a form of migration can seem ethereal and elusive, for how do we quantify what it means for a large population to see things anew and to begin to build social and cultural practices accordingly?

One of the remarkable features of the Harlem Renaissance is that its development ran parallel to the Great Migration, which lasted from 1910 to 1930. As blacks sought a new place to call home, the moment in the uptown Manhattan area known as Harlem was ripe for renewal. Though today, Harlem is synonymous with black life and presence, it wasn't always so. Rather, Harlem was a portion of Manhattan whose origins were Dutch and that subsequently hosted Irish and Jewish communities. Though representing different ethnicities, the neighborhood had historically been a predominantly white enclave of Manhattan. This began to change in the early 1900s when, during a particularly soft housing market, enterprising black realtors, such as Philip A. Payton, began to encourage white property owners to take on black tenants, who would be willing to pay higher rents on a timely basis, all while taking good care of the apartments they kept. Despite the prevalence of overt racism at the time, the offer typically proved too enticing and practical to resist, even if the established white tenants resented their white landlords for the influx of blacks into their buildings. Harlem's swift and decisive transition to a haven for blacks, or a City of Refuge as David Levering Lewis coined it in his authoritative study of the Renaissance, was remarkable. So much so that those involved and present could sense a historic moment was on the horizon.[2] In 1925, James Weldon Johnson marveled:

> In the make-up of New York, Harlem is not merely a Negro colony or community, it is a city within a city, the greatest Negro city in the world. . . . It has its own churches, social and civic centers, shops, theaters and other places of amusement. And it contains more Negroes to the square mile than any other spot on earth. . . . There is nothing just like it in any other city in the country, for there is no preparation for it; no change in the character of the houses and streets; no change, indeed, in the appearance of the people, except their color.[3]

It is easy from our contemporary vantage point to overlook the significance of this change, but consider that the Emancipation Proclamation freeing black slaves had only been in effect some fifty years or so and that, just as importantly, Reconstruction had proven to be a failure. Meanwhile, Ida B. Wells was in the final years of a life devoted to fighting lynching but without realizing compelling effective legislation and state protection for blacks. This left lynching and racial violence standing as clear and distinct features of American society and democracy. It was in the face of these circumstances that blacks secured for themselves a geographical slice of one of the wealthiest cities in the world. The Great Migration was instrumental in supplying Harlem with many of its new denizens—but another migration, of a spiritual kind, was getting underway, and it had both a spokesperson and visionary.

Alain Locke was born September 3, 1885, in Philadelphia. More than a biographical factoid, his date of birth is important, for it suggests a person with a powerful intellect and presence, since Locke was in his mid-thirties when the Harlem Renaissance began to make its significance known. As the first black American to win a prestigious Rhodes Scholarship while an undergraduate at Harvard during a time when almost no blacks attended Ivy League institutions, it likely surprised very few people that Locke rose to become an intellectual leader in the black community. What appears more notable is that in the wake of Reconstruction's failure, Locke urged black Americans to double down on American democracy. Marcus Garvey had recently mounted a powerful and widely known national campaign for blacks to return to Africa with the support of the intellectually gifted Hubert Harrison, a West Indian immigrant who earned his brief yet undeniable notoriety as a street corner scholar and orator. Locke's contemporary, the black sociologist and historian W. E. B. Du Bois, had also argued for such faith in the democratic tradition, albeit in a qualified manner. What set Locke apart from his peers and predecessors was the articulation of a refreshed model of black personhood he coined the "New Negro." And a truly exciting, and, as I will try to make clear, radical feature of his call for a refreshed model of black personhood was his belief in the role art ought to play, not merely as helpful for his vision, but as central and fundamental to the vitality of black social, economic, and political uplift.

What did Locke mean to signify by the term, the "New Negro"? To our ears today it sounds not only distinctly out of date but possibly counterproductive to racial reconciliation, since it suggests an essentialist view about what a black person ought to be. And such an essentialist vision constricts the possibilities for identity, since there is an ideal sort of blackness we each must strive to represent in our daily actions and habits. Locke, however, wasn't concerned with what it was to *be* a black person so much as he wanted to compel black Americans to reimagine the way they *saw* the world and their place in it *as* black people. The difference between the preoccupation over how to be black and how to best envision a flourishing black life is crucial for understanding two ways in which the Harlem Renaissance was indeed a moment of black radicalism and not only an era to be romantically recalled for its outstanding literature, music, poetry, drama, and art.

The radical potential of Locke's thinking was sketched in what many consider to be the defining piece of writing for the Renaissance, Locke's lead essay in a special volume he edited in 1925, *The New Negro*. There were two strands of radical potential. The first was that Locke wanted black Americans to form for themselves a refreshed picture of their place in American society, outside the strictures of white supremacy, and to appreciate more powerfully the resources in their heritage that could help actualize that picture. Only two decades earlier, in his pathbreaking and enduring work *The Souls of Black Folk*, Du Bois had established the color line as America's greatest problem. Du Bois offered a psychological argument about the burden of double consciousness for blacks—to see the world through both black eyes and white eyes. This double consciousness left blacks with an unsteady psychological perspective, thus, a sense of self that could achieve steadiness but only at the costs imposed by a white supremacist society and political structure.

Locke chose to bypass psychological arguments that focused on obstacles and predicaments, which is not to say he disagreed with those arguments. Rather, invoking a more enterprising and aspirational spirit in the essay, Locke settled squarely on seeing the world through blacks' eyes and what ought to inform their vision of the past, present, and future. He wrote:

> The Negro to-day is inevitably moving forward under the control largely of his own objectives. What are these objectives? Those of his outer life are happily already rather well and finally formulated, for they are none other than the ideals of American institutions and democracy. Those of his inner life are yet in process of formation, for the new psychology at present is more of a consensus of feeling than of opinion, of attitude rather than of program.[4]

Notice that Locke did not open room for debate on what blacks wanted from America clearly, they wanted inclusion and democratic acceptance. The more fraught as well as promising part of the racial sociopolitical equation had to do with blacks' relationship with themselves. Specifically, Locke thinks that blacks' inner self-definition offers a moment for creativity guided by the looseness but gravity of shared opinions and attitudes, rather than by the cohesiveness but formality of political agendas. He continued, "the Negro to-day wishes to be known for what he is, even in his faults and shortcomings, and scorns a craven and precarious survival of seeming to be what he is not."[5]

If Locke's views strike you as gesturing toward a creative moment for black Americans at a fraught time, then his words have hit their mark. It has become vogue for commentators to suggest that American democracy is a project in the making rather than a triumph finalized by independence from the English crown and the subsequent establishment of our Constitution more than two centuries ago. Locke, however, was distinctive in pinning blacks' political hopes and democratic aspirations to their artistic output. Locke observed, "It does not follow that if the Negro were better known, he would be better liked or treated. But mutual understanding is basic for any subsequent cooperation and adjustment."[6] This led Locke to what we might consider the condensed manifesto for the Renaissance:

> In the intellectual realm a renewed and keen curiosity is replacing the recent apathy; the Negro is being carefully studied, not just talked about and discussed. In art and letters, instead of being wholly caricatured, he is being seriously portrayed and painted.
>
> To all of this the New Negro is keenly responsive as an augury of a new democracy in American culture. He is contributing his share to the new social understanding.[7]

Locke's gambit was not to make black art profitable, thus enabling blacks to enter American society as equals through the back door of wealth and status. He instead insisted that black art could help remediate one of America's greatest failures—the disvaluation of black lives, the prevalent sense that black lives were inconsequential and disposable. In his own words: "The especially cultural recognition they win should in turn prove the key to that revaluation of the Negro which must precede or accompany any considerable further betterment of race relationship."[8]

Locke's momentous groundwork helped establish a politico-cultural timbre for the times. Retrospective considerations of a person's historical importance frequently run the risk of overemphasizing his or her importance to a moment. And, to be sure, it would be slightly extravagant to nominate Locke as the "founder" of the Renaissance. All the same, there is something to be said in favor of his being a central pillar of the era, if not its founder. Historian Jeffery Stewart offered the following observation:

> The creativity of the New Negro in [the 1920s] reflected a pivotal transitional moment in American history when the old rural agricultural world was disappearing and a new, alien, yet still communal, northern, industrial world was taking its place. In that process, black identities, like white ones, were freed from the old constraints on individualism and group consciousness that the old "medieval America," as Locke put it, had imposed on southern Americans, black and white. That transition brought a great deal of nostalgia, but also a greater idealism that anything was possible for the culturally self-conscious black personality.[9]

Stewart is correct in pointing out that the years of the Harlem Renaissance were remarkable nationally for many reasons for whites as well as blacks. But he is also correct to suggest that there was something exceptional at stake for blacks. The moment of the New Negro, hitched to the arts though it was, represented a valuable and possibly fleeting opportunity for blacks to assert themselves as valuable citizens and democratic participants. Locke felt that blacks could do their part to make a cultural contribution to democracy; and that way of putting matters—thinking of democracy as a way of life rather than merely an organizational form of government—pivots us toward the second stream of radicalism the Renaissance represented. If the first kind was a disruptive way for blacks to re-evaluate their role in American life, the second kind came to be embodied in the very spirit of the word "renaissance."

That term—*renaissance*—is usually reserved for acknowledging or marking a cultural resurgence of a group, population, or nation. The idea of a Harlem Renaissance should strike you as odd. What, exactly, was the resurgent feature of black American life supposed to be? The critical position of black intellectual leaders, long before Locke but certainly including him and those of his time, was that whites were guilty of systematically devaluing black lives by erasing and suppressing blacks' cultural history and traditions. Locke and those who participated in the vigorous cultural life of blacks during the Renaissance years sought to achieve a basic, yet essential goal—to represent blacks as worthy citizens by (re)presenting to whites' sensibilities the depth of black heritage and culture. Here, the resurgence is not necessarily intrinsic to what was happening for blacks on the ground so much as what was meant to be happening to the image of blacks in whites' minds—the image of blacks rising and imposing their cultural honor, prestige, and productivity on the wider society. This was maybe the most radical element of the Harlem Renaissance, to push whites to not merely acknowledge that blacks should be seen as bearers of rights, for example, but that they should be seen that way because they were the bearers of human souls rich in history and culture. Locke would help mightily some of black America's most treasured minds and the finest talents to have ever graced us with a word on a page, a note for our ears, a brush stroke for our eyes. It is no use cataloging what turns out to be an immense body of work by a formidable cast of contributors during the Renaissance. Rather, let us focus on two individuals who sought not only to further Locke's aims but also to amend them, sometimes in direct opposition to Locke's vision. But this seems to me poetically proper. What is the point of urging self-determination if not to also accept the possibility of competing energetic and varied interpretations of how best to realize a self in a world that is at best ambivalent about your value, and at worst, seeking to erase you from that world?

It was without a trace of irony that a young Langston Hughes wrote in May of 1923—the early dawn of the Harlem Renaissance—in a letter to Alain Locke, "You are right that we have enough talent now to begin a movement. I wish we had some gathering place for our artists,—some little Greenwich Village of our own."[10] The poet, essayist, and novelist was himself a young and emerging talent but did not yet have the presence we today recognize him to have in the history of black arts and letters. His words to Locke are revealing. They intimate a knowledge of Locke's vision for the near future of black arts. But more tellingly, Hughes's words also suggest that even by 1923, the idea that Harlem's cultural producers would be globally and historically significant was yet to be widely accepted or perceived. And, of course, an especially poignant aspect of Hughes's unknowingly making a historic prediction by taking a stance of uncertainty is that he would be one of the more pivotal personalities of the Renaissance.

Hughes's own ascent had begun, maybe unknowingly to him, two years earlier when *The Crisis*, a magazine of black life and politics edited by W. E. B. Du Bois, published his poem "The Negro Speaks of Rivers." It was Hughes's second professionally published poem and, in many ways, spoke most powerfully to the idea of a black renaissance as a (re)presentation to whites of the depth of blacks' cultural

resources. It was also an invitation to blacks to recontextu-
alize their own historical importance. In the poem, Hughes
invoked African rivers as both historical and conceptual
tools. On the one hand, rivers like the Euphrates and Nile
are powerfully evocative of ancient natural forces in Africa
that have the power to sustain as well as to wreak havoc. On
the other, they are symbolic—they play a role in representing
Africanness and nobility; they ground the historical presence of black peoples and their lands of origin.

When he wrote, "I bathed in the Euphrates when dawns
were young,"[11] Hughes wanted the reader to imagine him
transported to a primeval time. Maybe he meant to also
invoke women and men's innocence from that epochal
construct we refer to as "Western civilization." One thing,
however, is clear. Hughes wanted this primeval time to
establish the presence of blacks as historically extended and
continuous: "I heard the singing of the Mississippi when
Abe Lincoln went down to New Orleans[.]"[12] In bringing to
mind the image of an American river Hughes made black
presence geographically local to readers. And, crucially,
by placing himself in the same time as Lincoln, he meant
to invoke the notion that the Great Emancipator was traveling alongside him. When it is all put together, it is very
little wonder Hughes's poem gained him such acclaim.
"The Negro Speaks of Rivers" was a thirteen-line exercise
in recasting the foundational presence of blacks in history
and noting that being in America, they were now in a place
whose defining feature supposedly was freedom and liberty.
In placing Lincoln in such close proximity to the scenes of
African and American rivers, Hughes signaled that he, as an
artist, was empowered to speak to the political problem of
racial emancipation because he, by way of his heritage, had

been a proud human before Lincoln, and certainly ought to be a respected one after.

Despite the poem's success in putting Hughes on the Renaissance map, his writing style subsequently pivoted in a different direction. He became specifically preoccupied with representing the rhythm and texture of everyday, common black life in order to pay that life its due respect, to honor it. Rather than continuing to develop the Western elegiac tone he had previously put to effective use, Hughes embraced the blues and jazz as the black art forms most worthy of his and other black artists' attention and inspiration. Importantly, Hughes's shift was a response to two slightly elder luminaries, Countee Cullen and his at times spiritual patron, Alain Locke, the man to whom Hughes wrote in the spring of 1923 that he agreed a movement was afoot.

Maybe the sharpest and most enduring of Hughes's writings marking out what I am claiming is his democratic theory of the common people can be found in an essay he wrote for *The Nation* in 1926, "The Negro Artist and the Racial Mountain." Though he never mentioned him by name, Hughes took his literary compatriot Cullen to task for having once remarked that he desired to be a poet rather than a "Negro" poet. Hughes clearly took this as an affront, not to himself personally, mind you, but to the idea and fact of black identity against the backdrop of American history. What were Hughes's grievances, and what motivated them? He saw Cullen's denial of "Negro" as a worthy and desirable predicate for a description of his art as a betrayal. Hughes considered the rejection of that predicate to be tantamount to a wholehearted embrace of another descriptor: white. This would not do for Hughes. Such an embrace distanced black artists from not only their heritage, but, very essentially, the

common folk Hughes loved, revered, and thought fundamental to the cultural health of black arts. These black lives—
the ways and means of everyday black folk—mattered deeply
to Hughes. Hughes wrote in his essay, "These common people are not afraid of spirituals, as for a long time their more
intellectual brethren were, and jazz is their child. They fur-
nish a wealth of colorful, distinctive material for any artist
because they still hold their own individuality in the face of
American standardizations."[13] The concluding words of this
sentence are key, especially as we think about the relationship of Renaissance thinkers to the slogan of the day, "black
lives matter."

The "low-down" people, as Hughes referred to what we
would today call "everyday" or "lay" people, had an edge on
the cultural cognoscenti. Scholars like Locke and Du Bois had
made the study of black culture the focus of their intellectual
lives and, in so doing, had made black culture unnecessarily intellectualized in Hughes's estimation. Of course, the
low-down folk didn't have the time or resources for research
and ruminations. They worked, when and if they could, and
then played, how and where their lives permitted. The main
form of play, of course, was cultural consumption, especially
music.[14] But because the low-down "are the majority"[15] and
"accept what beauty is their own without question[,]"[16] they
are more reliably in touch with what constitutes urgent and
relevant art, for they simply respond to art as a stimulus in
the midst of lives burdened by systemic racism, a feature
of the world that placed more burdens in the daily lives of
blacks than democracy removed. For Hughes, the proof was
in the contentment art provided the people. This led him to
insist that jazz and the blues represented "the tom-tom revolt
against weariness in a white world[.]"[17]

There is something else worth appreciating in Hughes's proclamation. Seeing the low-down folks as the majority, and measuring their embrace of individuality and rejection of standardization, Hughes deftly addressed (though did not entirely resolve) one of the long-standing near-paradoxes in theories of democracy: the importance of the masses in identifying what is good for the people and the moral significance of the individual as a singular unit within the people. Rightly or wrongly, Hughes suggested that the low-down get it right because their judgments issue directly from the values and cues provided, used, and discarded in the course of living typical everyday lives, filled with challenges and triumphs, despair and hope as they may be. Hughes's landmark poem "The Weary Blues" indicated both his tonal shift and full embrace of this philosophical shift. Where "The Negro Speaks of Rivers" formally resembles a familiar European-style poem, "The Weary Blues" established a cadence clearly influenced by the swing of jazz music. The poem also employed a lingo mirroring the feel and mood of the blues. But the poem is not only a stylistic triumph. Hughes accomplished his ideal—to love and revere the music and the people who love the music in return.[18]

> Droning a drowsy syncopated tune,
> Rocking back and forth to a mellow croon,
> I heard a Negro play.
> Down on Lenox Avenue the other night
> By the pale dull pallor of an old gas light
> He did a lazy sway . . . .
> He did a lazy sway . . . .

Hughes's readiness and willingness to embrace the common folk, however, was unsurprising. Having been one of the fortunate few black youths whose parents had managed to be middle-class Americans at the turn of the century, Hughes was expected by his father to become a respectable professional. It was after much haggling that he got his father to allow him to matriculate at Columbia University to pursue a degree in engineering, which he never did complete. What is important to Hughes's story is that he seemed to always have rejected perceived elitism in favor of a more sensual life—a life marked by sights and sounds rather than by hypotheses and propositions. It is this feature of Hughes that no doubt led him to live a life on the sea as a crewman for many months in the early 1920s, before making Harlem his home.

Though Hughes relished the common life in his public pronouncements and published work and also endorsed a "non-intellectual" life in his many private letters, often saying that he preferred the life of the stupid to any other (and often, especially to Locke, wondered that he himself might be stupid), he was an incisive commentator on social and political matters. Whereas Jean Toomer's sensation *Cane* reimagined the form of the novel and revisited the narrative of slavery, and Jessie Fauset's *Plum Bun* explored themes of racial passing as well as homosexual love and affection, Hughes leveraged his championing of the lay American to challenge the very idea of who counted, who mattered as an American.

In another landmark poem, "I, Too," Hughes was particularly concerned with making good on the ideal of the New Negro. Though he might have had differences with Locke on the importance of jazz to black culture and thereby American culture, Hughes never seemed to waver on the more basic and essential ideal of the movement set out by his mentor: to identify, consume, and help produce robust cultural resources to help serve as a bulwark against the forces of white supremacy that made their presence and power felt with every lynching and Jim Crow train car. To emphasize this role of the Renaissance and its stable of socially and politically motivated culture producers, Hughes began his poem with the line, "I, too, sing America."[19] This line not only affirms the voice of the speaker as he states his ability to sing, but, more importantly, declares that a person can sing the ideal of a nation, can vocalize the aspiration of liberal democracy. In the poem, this aspiration takes the form of basic recognition and inclusion. The black speaker in the poem is banished a couple lines later to a separate space by his white friends or employers when their acquaintances show up for social gatherings, but shrugs off the disparagement and resolves, "Tomorrow, / I'll be at the table / When company comes."[20] At first, this seems mere resistance, a rejection of being cast off as so much unwanted debris. But the following lines recast this resistance into something more glorious: "Besides, / They'll see how beautiful I am / and be ashamed."[21] The speaker moves from resistance to self-affirmation. But much more crucially recognizes two capacities in those who have disparaged him. That they could, if they tried, see in him what he sees—beauty. Maybe more hopefully, they can feel shame, a sense of needing to engage in moral redemption for having failed to see his beauty in the first place. And in seeing his beauty, the speaker can assert equality: "I, too, am America." In moving from vocalizing the ideal to embodying it, Hughes affirmed the radical aim of the Renaissance to present to white Americans what had been true all along: that blacks are humans worthy of respect and dignity, that black lives matter.

***

Though today we tend to look back on creative luminaries like Hughes as constituting an elite class of artists, a remarkable feature of the Renaissance was the number of writers, artists, and musicians who genuinely endeavored to represent "the people." This term should be appreciated in two senses. In the first place, there is an ethnic use of "the people," as when people say, "black folks are my people." A person saying this affirms a sense of solidarity motivated by identity: a shared appreciation of certain foods, the cohabituation of particular social norms, and an ear for local vernacular, for example. But there is also a more abstract and democratic sense of "the people"—the group constituting the polity over whom a government will exercise power. Indeed, what is supposed to make democracy such a powerful and just form of governance is that it is the very people over whom power is exercised that political elites must appeal to in attaining political office. We saw in Hughes both senses at work. His pivot toward jazz and blues sensibilities signaled a full embrace of "the people" in the ethnic sense; his notion that the people should have power over art because they constitute the many who will consume it signaled his democratic sensibilities. But Hughes was not alone in his convictions; and such convictions could express complementary yet distinct visions of what it meant to invoke "the people." We will consider Hurston's vision for, as Hazel Carby puts it, Hurston "epitomized the intellectual who represented 'the people' through a reconstruction of 'the folk.'"[22]

Zora Neale Hurston hailed from the South. Though census records indicate that she might have been born in Alabama, Hurston consistently claimed Eatonville, Florida, as her home. Hurston was not the only Renaissance migrant to New York, but she was one of the migrants who most powerfully sought to represent the folk tradition of black Americans. Though Hughes was right to insist on the relationship between the "low-down" people and blues, it should be remembered that the jazz and blues themselves had roots in traditional black music. While jazz and the blues were often considered raw and sometimes even untamed, it was still the case that these genres came to represent refinements of folk music. Indeed, people made studies out of being a jazz musician, and this was in part due to the music's growing commercial status. Historic black folk music and storytelling, however, tended to remain firmly in the hands of local practitioners, many of them in the South. Hurston embraced making the voice of these traditions, as her artistic and political vocation, integral to Alain Locke's New Negro movement.

Today, Hurston remains most closely identified with her important and groundbreaking book *Their Eyes Were Watching God*. The landmark novel tells the story of Janie Crawford's life as a woman who, in search of contentment, instead bears the burden of racism and misogyny in addition to a hurricane-caused flood of epic proportions. Janie's character is powerful. She displays and affirms the authority of a woman's agency in making her own choices and expressing her sexuality—a portrayal that was unusual among representations of black women characters. It is also significant that Janie outlives both her husband, Jody, who proves to be oppressive and abusive, as well as the biblical flood that is the cause of so much death around her, including that of her final, younger lover in the book *Tea Cake*. In making Janie the last woman standing, Hurston makes her a self-resilient survivor in the face of conditions that oppress many. However, *Their Eyes Were Watching God* was published in the final days of the Renaissance, so in many ways it represents a culmination of Hurston's efforts to synthesize the ethics of the New Negro movement with her commitment to her own vision of the power of the people. I want to explore two ways we can appreciate Hurston's own sense of radical black politics through art.

The first entry is appreciating that in many ways Hurston took herself to be a performative representation of black affirmation and self-possession. One of Hurston's major endeavors was to travel across America collecting folklore. In this she found support over the years from both private benefactors, including Charlotte Osgood Mason, as well as from the government in its support of public works programs in President Roosevelt's New Deal policies. A result of Hurston's extensive travels and research was a volume of black folkloric inspired writing, *Mules and Men*, as well as a stage production, *The Great Day*. I will return to these pieces as part of the second way we might appreciate Hurston's importance to the Renaissance and enduring power for affirming black life and culture. But first, especially with Hurston, it is key that we observe the person behind the art, since for her, having a black life that mattered was as much about the act of self-creation as it was about the art that flowed from self-creation.

Maybe one of the most remarkable and inspiring things about Hurston is what can only be described as her indomitable spirit. In black intellectual life and writing to this day, it is quite common and appropriate for black Americans to lament the abuses of racism, the real costs in terms of money as well as measured by the tragic loss of black lives. Hurston operated differently. She often chose to focus on the glory of a lived life. Do not be mistaken. Her affirmations were not naïve—she was as aware as anyone else that life in America was often perilous for black Americans. Yet Hurston thought it paramount that one act as a force of affirmative will rather than under the thumb of racial oppression. Thus states her playful yet utterly serious proclamation, "Sometimes, I feel discriminated against, but it does not make me angry. It merely astonishes me. How *can* any deny themselves the pleasure of my company! It's beyond me."[23] Hurston was equally strident in speaking about her ability to continue discovering and making her self: "I am not tragically colored. There is no great sorrow dammed up in my soul, nor lurking behind my eyes. . . . Even in the helter-skelter skirmish that is my life, I have seen that the world is to the strong regardless of a little pigmentation more or less. No, I do not weep at the world—I am too busy sharpening my oyster knife."[24]

Hurston's disposition to racial animus and prejudice was purposeful and ethical. Its purpose was clear: to provide a model of the self-possessed woman, much in the spirit of Emersonian self-affirmation. Such a person was not self-possessed due to narcissism or arrogance. Rather, one's self-possession was a natural consequence of recognizing one's own humanity, of paying homage to one's own possibilities and potentialities. The ethical aspect of Hurston's disposition is not as crisply explicit, but it is no less significant. For Hurston, self-possession was part of what it meant to deal with the world truthfully and to promote a more capacious vision of black humanity. For example, Hurston was deeply critical of white allies (or black ones, for that matter) who felt that black testimony about what it meant to be black in America was inauthentic if it didn't focus on portraying pain and suffering. In Hurston's words, "It has been so generally accepted that all Negroes in the South are living under horrible conditions that many friends of the Negro up North actually take offense if you don't tell them a tale of horror and suffering. They stroll up to you, cocktail glass in hand, and say, 'I am a friend of the Negro, you know, and feel awful about the terrible conditions down there.' That is your cue to launch into atrocities amidst murmurs of sympathy."[25] Here Hurston thinks two important things are going wrong. On the one hand, those consuming that testimony are not doing so to genuinely learn anything new about black Americans. Rather, they already have concluded that their condition is wretched and merely seek confirmation. The democratically dangerous thing here is that the process of mutual understanding is colonized by the listener's false commiseration—a commiseration the falseness of which is masked by utterances like "I am a friend of the Negro, you know." Except that real friends seek to comprehend the life of another rather than desire the narrative of another's life to bolster their own sense of goodness. Of course, the other thing that goes wrong here is that the black testimony provider who appeases such an expectation truncates her own humanity by demoting her own capacity for joy and hope—she victimizes herself doubly by being complicit in this democratically damaging exchange and by limiting her own possibilities for grasping her own humanity.

And this is why Hurston's work on reclaiming, excavating, and recovering the ways of black folk traditions was essential. Black folk traditions contained markers of overlooked black history, and such traditions were intrinsically substantively rich. But over and above everything else, they presented alternate modes of black agency in the value assigned to storytelling in various mediums, from lying contests to weaving tales on one's porch, to folk music such as black spirituals. This is our second way of appreciating

Hurston's place in the Renaissance and the lessons she imparts to modern social movements.

In a letter to Langston Hughes, dated April 12, 1928, Hurston queried the person she sometimes addressed as "Dear Pal" with the following proposition: "Did I tell you before I left about the new *real* Negro art theatre I plan? Well, I shall, or rather *we* shall act out the folk tales, however short, with the abrupt angularity and naivete of the primitive 'bama nigger. Just that with naïve settings. What do you think?"[26] It can at first be a bit shocking to hear someone like Hurston— a proponent of black uplift—speak in these terms. Notice, if you will, the equivocation between the idea of being a "real Negro" and a 'bama Nigger [Alabama nigger—colloquialism for a black person from the rural parts of the Deep South] and the connotations that such a black person would be naïve. Initially, Hurston's proposition can seem demeaning, insulting, even exploitative. But this is to misunderstand Hurston's manner of honoring black folk traditions. Rather than condescending, Hurston meant to persuade Hughes that the folk traditions she had been and remained interested in studying represented something basic, maybe even more pure in black culture than competing expressions of black culture.

Of these competing expressions, Hurston was especially suspicious of commercialized, black folk art and traditional spirituals. For example, Hurston was circumspect about the Fisk Jubilee Singers, who had made such a name for themselves in the public singing of black spirituals that they spent many months on a tour that stretched around the globe. For Hurston, something of the rawness and spontaneity of expression in black folk art was lost when it was expressed as a commercial product. Crucially, this is the context for making sense of Hurston's proposition to Hughes. When she invokes the idea of the naïve 'bama Nigger she is doing quite the opposite of being patronizing or insulting. Instead, acts like the Fisk Jubilee Singers, so far as Hurston was concerned, were the cause of the misrepresenting of what is genuine and good about black art. They were being irresponsible in letting the white world believe that the essence of Negro art is a commodity that can be reproduced by professional outsiders for the benefit of those who reside even further outside the bounds of black life than the Fisk singers: "Hurston rejected the mainstream New Negro surrogation of the folk spirituals as a harmful appropriation performed for the sake of middle-class uplift and a misguided narrative of cosmopolitan evolution."[27] For Hurston, such an appropriation ran counter to an important purpose of folk art: to speak the voice of the people in order to strengthen the possibility of the democratic bond, or at least, one source of popular expression that is meant to be a part of democratic exchange.

So, then, what of Hurston's proposition to Hughes? If she was set on securing the voice of the folk and doing so as genuinely as possible, what did her efforts come to? An underappreciated facet of Hurston's legacy is her personal investment in black theater—and by personal investment, I mean the mostly profitless endeavors she seemed to tirelessly undertake for the sake of bringing to a wider audience what she assessed to be a more appropriate rendering of black folk life. The most prominent of these efforts was a stage play, *The Great Day*. Its subject matter was mundane and basic in a manner fitting to the aspiration to authenticity—it represented one day in the life of black railroad workers. Nothing more, nothing less. Maybe one of the more intriguing aspects of this effort is that it postdates a failed collaboration between Hurston and Hughes, whom she had four short years earlier petitioned to join her in an effort to produce art for the theater. The two writers had for some time been co-writing a play we know today under the title *Mule Bone*. There are some conflicting senses of why the collaboration failed, and maybe the most widely accepted story conveys the likelihood that Hurston felt Hughes was insufficiently flexible in his artistic license to grant her the creative space she needed to ground the authenticity of their joint endeavor. Whether or not this is exactly true, it is nevertheless interesting that the production that *did* make it to theater was steeped in the very local and mundane lives of railroad workers.

Maybe more essentially, Hurston's and Hughes's ambition shared a democratic sensibility even if they had not explicitly sought to promote some democratic theory. Though Hughes thought the majority of the people had it right about the power of jazz and the blues, Hurston's turn to folk art was not so much concerned with a consensus of black art as it was the underlying mechanics of black art. Though Hurston made a study of folk art, she was also a participant in a variety of settings. She acted and danced in many later iterations of *The Great Day*, and she participated in porch storytelling during her visits to Eatonville over the course of her research. On the one hand, such participation and her willingness to continuously reconsider the content and staging of *The Great Day* indicated her respect for the improvisational spirit of folk art. On the other, something even deeper is going on that is significant for acknowledging the democratic possibilities in Hurston's respect for black folk art. Anthea Kraut observed, "Without question, creativity in folk forms is cooperative in nature, relying heavily on the participation of an 'aesthetic community' of other performer-spectators. Yet it is equally evident that the manner in which intervention unfolds in vernacular arenas gives rise to an atmosphere in which practitioners try to outdo one another and continually vie for personal acclaim."[28] Really, what is democracy if not the tension, the continual dance between productive collaboration, on the one hand, and personal gain and stability, on the other? What is ethically significant about democratic life, though, is not that this tension exists. This seems a necessary state of affairs for any society that makes personal liberty a condition of establishing a general and public will. What is ethically significant about this view of democracy as embodied in the collaborative efforts of folk art is the presumption of equality—that each participant is an equal and equally legitimate coproducer of the final product as well as an equally entitled stakeholder in renegotiating the shape and substance of the final product. In other words, a genuine democracy takes for granted that each voice matters because politics—the final product— affects each life.

From this point of view, it is much easier to appreciate that Hurston took herself to be a legitimate coproducer of the conditions for a fair democracy, and precisely because blacks had still not achieved full formal equality, we ought to appreciate her radicalism as consistent with the general radical aims of the Renaissance. Maybe Hurston was more radical, given her ambition to dig deeper into the roots of black life, than Alain Locke or Langston Hughes (despite his love for the "low-down"). It could be that Hurston was after a different, more ethically charged conception of the "low-down":

No one of darker skin [on account of Jim Crow] can ever be considered an equal. Seeing the daily humiliation of the darker people confirm the [white] child in its superiority, so that it comes to feel it the arrangement of God. By the same means, the smallest dark child is to be convinced of its inferiority, so that it is to be convinced that competition is out of the question, and against all nature and God.[29]

In other words, Jim Crow denied the fundamental claim of blacks to their right to be coproducers of democracy, as well as their legitimacy in participating in its renegotiation. Societies, like persons, can develop bad habits as well as long memories that shape, influence, confound, and reproduce political outcomes. Maybe Hurston's explicit political claim in her artistic efforts as a leader of the New Negro movement should be taken as a cautionary tale of why today, more than eighty years later, we must insist that black lives matter.

The essence of radical politics is using unsanctioned means to effect change to disrupt the status quo. As the twentieth century settled into industrial post-Reconstruction life, blacks found themselves under the thumb of Jim Crow, just mere decades following the Emancipation Proclamation. The freedom promised by the proclamation decayed and devolved into a new, insidious imagining of black subservience. But oppression is rarely ever complete and absolute. In the early twentieth century, freedom from slavery at least enabled geographic mobility and some potent opportunities for commercial participation. Despite their sense of possibility or their desires to merely do the work for its own sake, black artists converged on uptown Manhattan and developed a cultural epoch that was indispensable for blacks and irresistible to whites. In the course of doing so, their convergence came to represent far more than a phenomenal and serendipitous confluence of history and human will. Rather, the exceptional individuals who made up the movement—many more than could be engaged in these pages—took it as their charge to produce more than art for art's sake. They created art for the sake of black humanity.

Which brings us back to Kendrick Lamar's performance more than eighty years after the Renaissance. Like his cultural forebears, Lamar had a distinct sense of the rebellious, radical possibility of art. Indeed, by standing on top of a demolished cop car in the wake of a series of brutal killings of black men and women by the police, Lamar sought to reappropriate the symbol of the cop car to disrupt the status quo. We might further consider Lamar's performance radical since many on the political right seemed to think his reappropriation was unsanctioned, that his reappropriation went afoul of proper public norms, that hip-hop as a black musical art form lacks legitimacy. For example, liberal-turned-conservative Geraldo Rivera said the following on Fox News on June 30 in the aftermath of Lamar's BET performance: "This is why I say that hip-hop has done more damage to African-Americans than racism in recent years. This is exactly the wrong message."[30] Of course, Rivera was not the first commentator to turn the tables on black art in the name of blaming the victim. Jazz music was commonly described as "hot" music during the Renaissance. In some quarters, rather than denote pace, tempo, and exuberance, this was meant to suggest sexual license. Duke Ellington—maybe jazz's most visionary large ensemble composer and another pillar of the Renaissance—was at times located at the center of claims that "hot" jazz was responsible for sexual licentiousness and even rape, though his main ambition was to write work that would one day be staged at Carnegie Hall, just as the white bandleaders whose music was of questionable quality and sophistication compared to Ellington's.

That such responses were lobbed at blacks who commanded a conversation that would promote their well-being according to the ethics of racial justice is unsurprising. The more surprising and tragic aspect is that when viewed from a certain perspective, Lamar seems historically interchangeable with Hurston and Hughes—they all advocated for black agency in order to bring integrity and balance to American democracy. The institutional structures that beget inequality, and the personal vices that are complicit in institutional injustice, would cease to be impediments if only they would redeem themselves consistent with the promise and ideal of a reasonably ordered democracy. Hughes and Hurston fought to produce and promote their art so that the debate over whether a black life matters would be moot in future generations. That debate, sadly, is not moot—rather, it is alive and urgent. This is all the more reason to appreciate that efforts like Lamar's do not stand on their own but rather on the shoulders of previous black artists, whose radical ambitions may not have been realized but also were not for nothing.

FOR OUR SONS, DAUGHTERS, AND

ALL CONCERNED SOULS

*This hatred and our anger are very different. Hatred
is the fury of those who do not share our goals,
and its object is death and destruction. Anger is a
grief of distortions between peers and
its object is change. Anger is
an appropriate reaction to racist attitudes, as is
fury when the actions arising from those attitudes
do not change.*
—AUDRE LORDE, *"Uses of Anger"*

ELEANOR BUMPURS WAS A MOTHER and grandmother.
She was arthritic and diabetic. Additionally, she suffered
from mental health issues when she was shot and killed in
her apartment in the Bronx, New York, on October 29, 1984.
Bumpurs was not murdered by an assailant attempting to
extract sellable goods from her apartment. Rather, she was
killed by a police officer while she was both naked and clearly
hysterical.

Bumpurs owed her landlord four months of back rent
totaling roughly $400. Over the course of attempts to collect,
Bumpurs claimed the improbable, that people were trying
to get into her apartment through the floorboards. She also
lodged other unlikely complaints. At no point did anyone

familiar with Bumpurs's proclamations attempt to secure help for her. Bumpurs's daughters seemed to miss her need for professional counseling and had suggested that she should refuse to open the door to anyone who came knocking. But, owing back rent as she did, someone was going to knock on her door eventually. On October 12, Bumpurs allowed building maintenance personnel into her apartment. They found no problems, other than cans of human feces sitting in her bathtub. The city sent a psychiatrist to assess Bumpurs on October 25, the determination being that she was psychotic. The recommended course of action was to evict her and then have her committed to a mental health facility.

On October 29, an NYPD Emergency Service Unit was sent to Bumpurs's apartment to try to talk her into coming out. Hysterical and distressed, Bumpurs refused. After drilling through her door lock to peer into her apartment, authorities observed that she was both naked and wielding a large kitchen knife. The police forced their entrance. At that point, Bumpurs struggled, and, despite the fact that she, a 66-year-old woman, was outnumbered six to one, an officer first blew off the fingers on one of her hands, and then unloaded his shotgun into her chest, fatally lodging nine pellets.

The Bumpurs case is tragically consistent with any number of police-related killings of black Americans, the crucial common factor being that in almost every instance the death seemed unnecessary; in each instance, it is clear that another outcome was genuinely possible. For example, in the Bumpurs case, it is painfully easy to imagine the police cutting a large enough whole in the door to facilitate shooting a tranquilizer at her. Clearly, her mental state did lead her to pose a potential threat. The pressing question in her case and in all cases of black lives being snatched by the state is this: why was the use of deadly force the required solution? Knowing that Bumpurs was both mentally troubled and at that moment dangerous, why did the police insist on aggressive tactics that were likely going to lead to a physical confrontation? A police officer making a physical threat against someone who seems dangerous is appealing to the aggressor's sense of self-preservation. But this strategy is only reasonable and likely to succeed when the aggressor is in a more or less rational state of mind. Authorities initiated the engagement with Bumpurs fully informed that she was far from rational; thus it should have been clear to all parties that no such appeal, implicit or explicit, was likely to result in a predictable and appropriate outcome.

But the Bumpurs case also raises another, often overlooked issue for us. Why was Bumpurs, an elderly black woman, especially vulnerable? So far as we know, she possessed no criminal record and was not in any sense known to be a violent person. How, then, did she find herself extinguished at the business end of a police officer's shot gun? The answer to that question depends on the historically and socially complicated relationship between race and gender. Bumpurs was a mother and grandmother who had entered her later years without adequate support for her mental health needs and, possibly, for her broader health needs. Despite the city's determination that she was not of sound mind, no plan was put in place to ensure a safe and orderly eviction. Her mental health status failed to motivate anyone to take the proper course of action to secure her personhood, her humanity. Indeed, in the aftermath, her personhood was erased and replaced with the picture of a person turned beast, as a statement from the Policemen's Benevolent Association grotesquely illustrated in a defensive media ad: "This 300-pound woman suddenly charged one of the officers with a 12-inch butcher knife, striking his shield with such force that it bent the tip of the steel blade."[1] But Eleanor Bumpurs was not a 300-pound force of nature. She was a black woman. This transformation of a black human into a dangerous beast was not the first, and eerily anticipated many other instances. For example, Eric Garner, a man choked to death by a New York police officer in public and on tape, was, notably, blamed for his own death because he was overweight. But Bumpurs's death as a black woman in need of care rather than brutality predates a different and more recent case that also ended in an unnecessary death.

On July 10, 2015, in Texas, Sandra Bland was stopped by Brian Encinia of the Waller County police department for failing to signal a lane change while driving her car. What ought to have been a routine stop and ticketing escalated into a confrontation. Footage captured from Encinia's patrol vehicle shows Encinia initially engaging Bland appropriately. After requesting her license and registration, Encinia reapproaches Bland's vehicle. Following a pause, he asks whether she is OK, and notes that she is agitated. Bland responds that she is irritated because she moved lanes because Encinia was driving too close behind her, and he now was giving her a ticket for her lane change. There is another pause, this time longer. Encinia then, oddly, asks Bland to put out her cigarette, even though she is sitting in her own car. This is where the trouble began. Bland refused, stating that she was sitting in her car and was not required to extinguish her cigarette. After a couple of exchanges, Encinia, agitated that Bland is challenging what seems an improper use of his authority, demands that Bland get out of her car. Again, she refuses, insisting that he provide her a rationale—none is forthcoming, other than his assertion that his command is lawful. He then attempts to physically remove Bland from the car, and after she successfully resists, he pulls back, draws his gun, and points it at her. Encinia marshals Bland to the sidewalk, where she lets loose a torrent of profanities and asks if he feels good about himself for pulling over a female for a lane change and pointing a gun at her. At this point, Encinia escalates the situation by forcing Bland, now cuffed, to the ground. Though this takes place out of the visual range of the dashcam, you can hear that Bland is made to feel pain. She tells Encinia that she is epileptic. Encinia's response? "Good." Three days later, on July 13, Bland was found hanging by a plastic bag from the ceiling of her holding cell.

In this case, unlike Bumpurs's and more recent cases, Bland was not killed by the hands of a law enforcement official. But, consistent with the death of Eleanor Bumpurs, neglect and the will to unnecessarily escalate a situation led to the death of a black woman. Bland had informed Encinia that she suffered from epilepsy and repeated this information when being processed after being arrested. Waller County prison did not have a mental health expert on hand, nor did it secure one over the days Bland was in custody. Why is this important?

Especially crucial in Bland's case, persons with epilepsy tend to be at higher risk of depression. Encinia's aggressive and violent escalation of what should have been a routine traffic stop introduced a trigger into Bland's life—she was humiliated and threatened by an agent of the state. But even if Bland had other reasons to commit suicide, the fact remains, she did not belong in that cell. What is sadly poignant about the series of events leading to Bland's death is that six months earlier, in January of 2015, she had begun to post videos in which she speaks out against police brutality in response to previous national stories of blacks being killed while in police custody and calling attention to the increasingly common fear among blacks that a person could die just by being stopped or confronted by a police officer. Bland, in effect, was a prophet of her own tragedy.

Eleanor Bumpurs's and Sandra Bland's unnecessary deaths are, of course, a source of criticism of police misconduct. But it would be incomplete and unfortunate to see these cases only in that light. Rather, Bumpurs and Bland were women who also clearly possessed vulnerabilities. Had these vulnerabilities been assessed and responded to with care and concern, both women would have gone on to live longer, hopefully healthier, maybe even happier lives. Instead, at pivotal moments of state confrontation, their humanity was put on hold and their vulnerabilities, in addition to their race, placed them in distinct danger.

The internal lives of black women have been much more complex than media, social movement leaders, or patriarchy at large have allowed us to see. But many powerful and brilliant women have championed the cause of women's acknowledgment and visibility. In doing so, they have pressed the case to white men, white women, black men, and even other black women that self-respect does not require women to deprive themselves of their emotional lives or intimate needs. Moreover, they have incisively challenged common and lazy understandings of identity formation and the political authority that is thought to arise from those understandings. A prevalent strand of thought in the black feminist tradition has sought to provide a vision of a better life for black women. One in which civil rights, freedom of sexuality, and economic liberation could all be front and center, for example. Of the many women who have done this, Anna Julia Cooper and Audre Lorde are worth special attention. Though separated in their writings and activism by more than a half-century, both women had a clear sense of the difficult social, political, sexual, economic, cultural terrain that stretched out before women in general, and the special challenges facing black women in particular. They took it as their vocation not merely to map this terrain in the name of caution, but to master it in the name of self-love and self-care.

Thirty-four years after Frederick Douglass faced the Ladies' Anti-Slavery Society in Rochester, New York, delivering his classic "What, to the Slave, Is the Fourth of July?" Anna Julia Cooper faced her own imposing audience to deliver an equivalent message urging contemplation and conscientious action. Two years fresh out of Oberlin College, Cooper delivered, in 1886, to the all-male black clergy of Protestant Episcopal Church, her speech "Womanhood: A Vital Element in the Regeneration and Progress of a Race." If Douglass's goal in his speech was to point out the hypocrisy and shame of white America's simultaneous celebration of personal democratic autonomy and national independence from a supposed despotic power while enslaving black Americans, Cooper's was at once more sublime and more penetrating. Cooper sought to insist that the very future of "the race" inextricably depended on greater respect for and liberty of black women; that in addition to the racism that clearly held blacks back, there was the additional historical offense of rendering black women inconsequential and politically invisible. As she wrote, "With all the wrongs and neglects of her past, with all the weakness, the debasement, the moral thralldom of her present, the black woman of to-day stands mute and wondering at the Herculean task devolving upon her." Thus, "the fundamental agency under God in the regeneration, the re-training of the race, as well as the groundwork and starting point of its progress upward, must be *the black woman*."[2] How is it that Cooper thinks we move from the entirely justified complaints of black women's mistreatment to the conclusion that the betterment of the race entirely depends on the improved position of black women?

The basic details opening Vivian M. Mays's biography of Cooper provide a very important initial clue. Mays observed, "Born into slavery in Raleigh, North Carolina in 1858, Anna Julia Cooper lived to be 105; she died just a few months before the signing of the Civil Rights Act of 1964."[3] Cooper's life spanned the dusk of the systematic ownership and exploitation of black people to the dawn of legal racial equality: the fading darkness of blacks being told when and where they could move through America, to the increasing brightness of the public resistance marches that forced a nation to face its historical demons. We can only imagine what life in America looked like to Cooper. Doing so with a bit of social attentiveness and sympathy, we can begin to understand how a black feminist came to be formed. The various struggles for black equality, including aspects of the Civil War, were a man's game, and as the twentieth century came around the historical bend, the most visible and sought-after race leaders were men—with whom Cooper sadly, but unsurprisingly, had difficult relationships.[4] It must have seemed to Cooper that even though blacks were in general treated poorly, black women were being consigned to the sidelines of the struggle by white *and* black men as well as by white women who were beginning to forcefully fight for women's rights with an inconsistent eye to the perils of racial oppression. Seen in this light, Cooper's position turns out to be not at all peculiar: a race cannot be said to advance while half of its population continues to be relegated to a subordinate status. But even this is not quite the whole explanation of Cooper's nuanced views.

Cooper is largely credited with being the first black feminist theorist.[5] It is striking for her time that she, being black and a woman, received a college degree from a school as elite as Oberlin. Cooper had read many of the important philosophers and historians of the day. Cooper's education and wide reading enabled an already fierce mind to avoid lazy assertion-making, thus when she told her black male audience, "A stream cannot rise higher than its source. The atmosphere of homes is no rarer and purer and sweeter than are the mothers in those homes[,]" she meant to convey more than the quaint and conservative notion that a woman's place in the home should be valued. Rather, she was, on the one hand, reflecting the tenor of her times. Keeping in mind that Cooper was making her address during the height of the Victorian era as well as the biographical fact that Cooper always considered herself a proper and mannered southern woman, we must understand that the preoccupation with the relationship between women and households is itself an artefact of the prevalent culture. This makes the other side of her intent all the more remarkable—despite the culturally conservative overtones of Cooper's commitment to the importance of black women to family structure, she meant to convey a sophisticated understanding of the structure of both government and civic education. Maybe surprisingly, it is the very structure of orthodox family and gender values that Cooper meant to call into question, in a manner anticipating Michel Foucault's mid-twentieth-century concerns with structural yet invisible power.[6] Consider this extended passage:

> The atmosphere of street cars and parks and boulevards, of cafes and hotels and steamboats is charged and surcharged with her sentiments and restrictions. Shop girls and serving maids, cashiers and accountant clerks, scribblers and drummers, whether wage earner, salaried toiler, or proprietress, whether laboring to instruct minds, to save souls, to delight fancies, or to win bread,—the working women of America in whatever station or calling they may be found, are subjects, officers, or rulers of a strong centralized government, and bound by a system of codes and countersigns, which, though unwritten, forms a network of perfect subordination and unquestioning obedience as marvelous as that of the Jesuits.[7]

This is a brilliant, poignant, and theoretically complex depiction of women's subordination—spending time appreciating the relationship between the various layers of power relationships in Cooper's scene is rewarding in its own right, but it will also help us get clear on the legacy of black feminism she left and that Audre Lorde, in particular, built something magnificent upon.

The first thing you should notice is the tension between a woman's station in life and her subordination. To the point, Cooper reveals that while a person would reasonably think her degree of autonomy and freedom would have some relation to her social position, such reason fails when and where women are involved—it matters little whether a woman works for a business owner or is herself a proprietor, for example. The next important conceptual point has to do with her putting in literal close proximity the idea of a centralized government and something less explicit, more amorphous, and deeply effective. Notice that Cooper places women in three possible sorts of relationships with a strong centralized government: subject, officer, or ruler. We may put these a bit more clearly as citizen, legislator, or governor or commander. At each level, a certain kind of recognition and authority is the proper provenance of that political identity. The citizen is entitled to the protection of the law and, in a democracy, of making contracts, voting, and consenting to the distribution of power. The legislator is meant to act in the people's interest by bringing to bear a certain amount and kind of bureaucratic expertise and an overarching knowledge of the working of government to expedite policies in that interest. Finally, the governor or commander is the embodiment of government to the people and for the people with respect to external powers. That person often has fairly expansive powers to determine the general direction of the development of the state. But despite the political place of each of these identities, Cooper tells us that the more essential identity is that of being a woman. And being a woman places one in a complex and problematic relationship with currents of power that undermine the logic of the prior political identities. More than undermine those identities, the authority that comes with each, limited as it may ultimately be, is rendered moot by the currents of power that define gender subordination.

Cooper says that women are "bound by a system of codes and countersigns, which, though unwritten, forms a network of perfect subordination and unquestioning obedience[.]" These signs and countersigns are a series of norms and expectations meant to structure women's behavior, such as the expectation that respectable women get married. This is a norm, as we will see below, that Cooper bucked, and her actions levied a toll on her career. What is very important about these norms—these codes and countersigns—is not that any one of them is meant to condition a woman's expectations, plans, or behavior. More alarmingly, it is important to note that they all hang together to create a social, political, and economic reality for women that serves to legitimate men's superiority over them: for example, women are more nurturing, so their job is to raise the children and manage the home's social affairs; women are overly emotional, so lack the cold rationality needed for politics; women are meek and naturally fit for childcare, so ought to withdraw from productive economic endeavors and remain in the home while men pursue their productive goals. We see the double burden black women faced and continue to face: the power of gender subordination and the power of racial subordination, which itself affirmed the preceding forms of suppression but also insisted that blacks were barely human at all; and because of that, their very lives were not their own to secure but instead were at the mercy of whites and the power they wielded.

Cooper provides her own testimony of the fraught and complex state of black social existence when she narrates the distinctive experiences of women traveling in America. She tells us that a group of young white women will be able to expect and, in fact, receive basic courtesies from the men they engage. For example, the train conductor is normally expected to help a woman with her bags and provide a stepping platform to ease the transition from the height of the train to that of the platform. But not so for black women. Rather, the conductors, "after standing at their posts and handing woman after woman from the steps to the stool, thence to the ground, or else relieving her of her satchels and bags and enabling her to make the descent easily, deliberately fold their arms and turn round when the Black Woman's turn came to alight."[8]

It seems to me we see more and more Cooper's nuanced endorsement of the importance of black women in the advancement of black people generally. Quite beyond the basic fact that black women give birth to black men, or that women are left to tend primarily to child rearing and home organization, black women's double oppression has provided them more lessons in the uses and abuses of power than it has anyone else—black men or white women.[9] We should appreciate, from a philosophical point of view, then, that Cooper was insightfully making the case that black women occupied a special epistemic place in American society—they knew America's sins because they experienced the wide variety of its vices, thus were in the most unique position to teach the proper virtues of emancipated citizenship.

This most likely accounts for the fact that, when asked about her vocation, in 1934, Cooper responded, "The education of neglected people." The power of Cooper's mind and the productivity of her pen took her across America and around the world to speak. Despite her commitments, including raising two foster and five adopted children by herself after her husband died, just a few months after they had married in 1877, Cooper's core mission was to be educated and to educate. This, tragically, posed a threat to status quo power holders, black and white.

In 1901, Cooper began what would turn out to be nearly a thirty-year tenure as principal of M Street High School in Washington, DC. During that time, one of her crowning achievements would be to insist that black minds mattered for black lives and for American democracy. This commitment drove Cooper to achieve something remarkable in securing accreditation for M Street. Prior to this feat, black students taught in black schools were able to apply to schools like Harvard University but were required to take an additional entrance exam—something not required of white students. The prejudiced thought was that even though blacks had received the requisite number of years of schooling, they likely had not received the "proper" *kind* of schooling. Cooper was clear that egalitarianism also applied to the capability of minds. She believed that even if it were true that blacks had not received the proper kind of schooling, it was a function of pedagogical vision on the side of black schools, which, in theory, was easy to change.

Cooper was, of course, correct that improving black students' performance could be as simple as changing the curriculum coupled with applying rigorous intellectual standards. But we must keep our historical bearings about us. Cooper was attempting this at the turn of the twentieth century. This was a time when America's—white America's—favorite race man was Booker T. Washington, a black leader famously and, in many black circles up to today, infamously known for advocating for the vocational education of blacks. He advocated for this so that blacks could bolster their income-earning power but not their intellectual, social, or political powers. More problematic was that in his Atlanta Compromise speech, delivered on September 18, 1895, Washington claimed to whites, "In all things that are purely social, we can be as separate as the fingers, yet one as the hand in all things essential to mutual progress."[10] This line is often considered tragic, since it is immediately preceded by Washington volunteering the black race to lay down their lives for whites in any war that might threaten America. It was without irony, then, that many blacks were concerned about what happens to fingers when hands form fists for the purpose of racist violence.

It is unsurprising, then, that Cooper's success at accreditation and the notable intellectual improvement she made in a black high school in the heart of the nation's capital were going to draw the wrong sort of attention: "Cooper's vision of Black education as being naturally on par with the full range of educational opportunities offered to white students was at odds with the powerful Booker T. Washington 'Tuskegee Machine,' particularly his narrow, conciliatory emphasis on a separate, unequal, and exclusively industrial educational paradigm."[11] Despite pressure from the District's Board of Education, which many contemporary commentators attribute to maneuvers on Washington's part, Cooper held firm. Her principled commitments, however, left her vulnerable—that word again—to an alternative campaign to make her comply with both the reigning white power structure and that of Washington's confused racial progressivism: she was accused of having a sexual relationship with John Love, who was both a student at M Street and one of Cooper's foster children. Despite Cooper's undeniable resilient character, a woman who prized southern properness and propriety as much as she did could ultimately only do so much to withstand the resentment articulated in what she must have found to be the painful but common deployment of the trope of the sexualized and sexually predatory black woman. She moved on, taking a position as an educator in Kentucky for five years before returning to M Street in 1910, when more reasonable minds prevailed.

In present times, a common refrain to the slogan "black lives matter" is the disingenuous retort, "all lives matter." This retort subverts the message of the original slogan by semi-sincerely worrying that to insist black lives matter must somehow mean that black lives matter more than other lives—in other words, those insisting that all lives matter are really concerned about what they perceive to be a fundamental inequality in the status of lives based on race. To these individuals it seems arbitrary that equality would be qualified by skin color. Of course, to most black observers, this is the height of bitter irony since the precise substance of saying "black lives matter" is to instate a nonarbitrary form of equality that eliminates the systematic endangerment of black lives, whether at the hands of the police by gunshot or at the welfare office through resource withholding. Anna Julia Cooper anticipated the roots of this debate quite clearly in her 1925 essay (amended in 1945), "Equality of Race and the Democratic Movement." In it, she reflects on the basic grounds of equality. She suggests that if there are such grounds it must have something to do with the very justification of democracy itself.

> Must we blame God because He made of one blood all peoples that dwell on earth but went to sleep during the firing when some millions were tanned yellow, some brown, and some even black .... The concept of Equality as it is the genuine product of the idea of inherent value in the individual derived from the essential worth of Humanity must be before all else unquestionably of universal application.[12]

Cooper, then, to the person who insists that all lives matter would express nothing but agreement. And she would ask in return, "[I]f all lives matter, then why don't *black* lives matter? Do you deny that blacks are humans? You likely do not, so you must then see that their differential treatment requires correction in favor of their humanity!"

This brings us back to the original puzzle we set for ourselves with respect to Cooper's seemingly conservative position on the centrality of black women to the improvement of the race.[13] We see much more clearly now that rather than conservative, her position was radical. Where women were consigned to subordinate status, Cooper sought to reposition black women as central to the very idea of racial progress. Were Cooper a present-day activist she would most certainly admire Alicia Garza, Patrisse Cullors, and Opal Tometi, the three black women who founded BlackLivesMatter.org. Their position has been that #blacklivesmatter must encompass black lives on both sides of the gender divide and across the spectrum of sexual identification. Cooper was one of the most important early feminist thinkers to argue that black women are worthy humans—their skin color was not a warrant for dehumanizing them; their sex was not a reason for rendering them invisible, mute, and usable. Given the ongoing issues of black women's invisibility despite formal gains in racial equality, I also think Garza, Cullors, and Tometi among many other women activists would in turn admire Cooper were she alive today to repeat one of her most enduring passages: "Only the BLACK WOMAN can say, 'when and where I enter, in the quiet, undisputed dignity of my womanhood, without violence and without suing or special patronage, then and there the whole *Negro race enters with me*.' "[14]

***

There are so many roots to the tree of anger
that sometimes the branches shatter
before they bear.

Sitting in Nedicks
the women rally before they march
discussing the problematic girls
they hire to make them free.
An almost white counterman passes
a waiting brother to serve them first
and the ladies neither notice nor reject
the slightest pleasures of their slavery.
But I who am bound by my mirror
as well as my bed
see causes in color
as well as sex

and sit here wondering
which me will survive
all these liberations.[15]

Despite the very real and deep issues Anna Julia Cooper experienced, witnessed, and theorized surrounding the dual problems of race and gender—the problems of black womanhood—Cooper approached the range and depth of these issues in an uncomplicated manner. I don't mean Cooper was unsophisticated; quite the opposite, we've seen that Cooper was quite analytically astute in dealing with the issues as she saw them. Yet for Cooper, the problem seemed to be that there were blacks and whites, men and women, and that there ought to be a way these four groups could be reconciled in the minds of Americans to recognize the moral claims arising from the fact that they are equal in humanity.

Audre Lorde's reaching imagination and personal experiences prompted her to articulate and face the problems of race and gender in a more complex register. Despite the discrimination Cooper faced because of her race and her gender, she was able to write and speak about both with ease insofar as they were widely accepted as salient identity categories. Audre Lorde, born February 18, 1934, in New York City—a city free from the quaint mores of southern life—came into the fraught world of white pride and racial prejudice just as Cooper was ending her thirty-year run at M Street. The ways of southern life, despite Cooper's worldliness, played a powerful role in her conceptions of virtue and decorum. Lorde's immediate world was comparatively both more progressive and more cosmopolitan. This facilitated her ability to go beyond Cooper in terms of the range of identities that she felt women had to define for themselves as well as urge others to recognize as morally serious. In particular, Lorde's feminism encompassed not only the politics of gender but also the politics of sex and sexuality. Despite being born into comparatively more progressive times, Lorde was still a pathbreaking theorist in her frank, intimate, and at times joyous and at other times painful explorations of queer sexual identity.

The fundamentals of Lorde's struggles are captured in the poem that opens this section, "Who Said It Was Simple?" The title is telling—it primes readers and listeners to question their own facile understanding of some thing. But what thing, exactly? Whatever the thing will turn out to be we are alerted in the first stanza that it is a thing that can have a close relationship to anger. The poem's structure is noteworthy because the first stanza stands on its own as a warning. Additionally, the arboreal metaphor suggests that the sources of anger are myriad and that anger's intensity can be stunting. The elegance in this verse is in the asymmetry it presents: myriad sources juxtaposed with singular intensity.

The second and longest stanza gracefully darts between the myriad sources of anger. The scene opens with a protest outside of what was one of New York's established eateries, Nedick's. That there is a protest suggests the presence of an injustice, thus the presence of complainants. But these complainants are discussing "the problematic girls that make them free." Here, it is most probable that these are white women discussing the black girls and women they hire to do their domestic chores, which was very common among middle-class and upper-class white households, especially during the time the poem was written and seems to be set. So, here we have women against women. But now notice that Lorde brilliantly layers another set of differences in the background: "an almost white counterman passes a waiting brother to serve the ladies first." This gives credence to the idea that the women are white. But very powerfully, it now expands the fields of contestability from intragender conflict to intraracial doubts—the counterman is "almost white," which means he is very light skinned but racially black; and because the man he passes is clearly a "brother," this means he is darker, so now the darker black man must not only suffer the indignity of being made to wait, but of being made to wait by one of his own who just happens to be much lighter. Lorde then shifts the scene back: the white women pay the black girls so that they can be free, yet they are slaves. How so? And if so, it must be a peculiar slavery since it has its pleasures. It is significant that these lines follow those depicting the almost-white counterman skipping over the brother to attend to the white women. Their pleasures are those of privilege, of being given priority in a society that debases blacks. But this does not make them free. Here, Lorde's point is moral. They pay the black girls so that they may be free to do as they please with their time and they get served first, but all this is only possible because they in fact are clearly dependent on the power their racial privileges bestow—none of the pleasures they enjoy are their own, and moreover, they are about to protest, most likely for women's rights. Lorde wants us to understand that these white women are ethically caught between white men's patriarchy and the system of white power on which they in fact have come to depend for the quality of their lives.

Now notice yet another shift. The poem begins with the impersonal and abstract, then moves to the more particular circumstances of four characters. Lorde then inserts herself. Lorde frequently used mirrors in her poems, and saw them as holding great poetic power since they only show us what is on the outside of the self. Thus they invite us to ask what is on the inside of the image the mirror represents as well as what is the character of a society that prompts us to care at all about what we see in that mirror. The mirror's role is especially important here, as it tells us one thing fairly reliably: whether we are white or black. Lorde claims she is bound by what she sees, but that is not all that binds her—she is also bound by her bed, which she uses to denote an erotic life and not just a gender-normed life. Many other things could have been used to denote gender oppression, such as marriage, which patriarchal norms associate with womanly "duties" of intimacy. Indeed, it was her sexuality in addition to her gender and race that prompted Lorde to reflect on what anchored her life experiences. And it was because she was bound by her race as well as her sexuality that she was able to see causes—reasons for social and political complaint—in both. Thus, these eight lines of the poem present the many cross sections of American society, illustrating that the simple categories of black and white, women and men, can no longer contain all that is important about identity politics.

The final three-line stanza makes concrete the abstract prophecy presented in the first three lines. Lorde wonders "which me will survive all these liberations[?]" She is worried about two things. One source of worry is that the complexity of identity on its own suggests that she is consigned to struggle to unify them under one canopy named "Audre Lorde." The other worry is that the issue isn't simply that Lorde could claim that she is a woman or a black person or a black woman or a lesbian or a black lesbian, but that each and every one of these categories in America often requires distinct struggles for full respect and recognition, and this takes a toll—how will she survive? Notice that now there is structural symmetry: three lines open the poem, three lines close the poem; a warning of the stunting power of anger opens the poem, a warning of being stunted by struggle closes the poem.

And struggle was something with which Lorde was acutely familiar. But even as the nature of Lorde's struggle was something she regarded as real and explicit, she thought that both the vagaries of struggle and the possibilities for redemption and flourishing that struggle introduces into our lives might be lost to mainstream interlocutors if presented in the guise of an orthodox autobiography. Thus, where most intellectuals may be wont to pen a straightforward autobiography, Lorde chose to categorize the story of her life as a "biomythography," a term she created for her own purposes in her book *Zami, A New Spelling of My Name: A Biomythography*. I suspect the creation was to give her literary space to represent the struggles she endured. The term suggests not just a story of a life but of a body; we have the idea not just of a recollection of a life but also its place in the pantheon of black lived experiences as shaped by the gods of justice and the demons of oppression.[16] The re-presentation of struggle begins for Lorde, I think, as with most precocious children, with relating her present and future to that of her parents' present and past, especially her mother's.

Consider the juxtaposition of two themes in the following passages. First, Lorde wonders over her attraction to positions outside the bounds of the usual or typical. She writes, "I have often wondered why the farthest-out position always feels so right to me; why extremes, although difficult and sometimes painful to maintain, are always more comfortable than one plan running straight down a line in the unruffled middle."[17] Then, just two lines later, the theme seems to shift suddenly: "My mother was a very powerful woman. This was so in a time when that word-combination of *woman* and *powerful* was almost unexpressable in the white American common tongue, except or unless it was accompanied by some aberrant explaining adjective like blind, or hunchback, or crazy, or Black."[18] Here, Lorde is involved simultaneously in a celebration and a lament. On the one hand, she admires her mother because she is a woman of presence and fortitude; on the other, she sees her mother's virtues as suppressed by the white world that cannot see a strong black woman as anything other than disabled or a "freak." It is telling that Lorde signals that being black was close enough to be being freak; being black certainly wasn't valued as part of normal humanity. Lorde, then, closely relates being most comfortable when thinking or acting outside the bounds of expected norms with being of two minds about her mother, who was normal in her virtues but whose virtues could never be accepted as normal to white Americans. It would become clear that Lorde prized her preference for non-normed thinking (and living) so as to avoid the charade her mother was implicitly forced to carry on, of being ordinarily extraordinary in a world that only saw her as peculiarly problematic.

Indeed, so problematic were blacks who insisted on occupying places where they normally did not belong that when the landlord of the building Lorde's family lived in committed suicide, her family was singled out as the cause, since it was presumed the landlord had hit such hard times that he had been forced to rent to blacks out of necessity. This was the narrative facing a young Audre as she was also the first black student at St. Catherine's School in New York. Lorde suffered from very poor eyesight, and was often presumed stupid because of it. Maybe more hurtful was the way her strong and proud mother relentlessly imbued Audre with the motivation and desire to work as hard as she could to preempt the failure Americans expected from blacks. It was such events, dynamics, and quandaries, which stretched not so lazily across black Americans' lives, that made Lorde ponder in "Who Said It Was Simple?" the causes of being a stunted person, of being frustrated with American life to such an extent that all a person managed to do was live to see another day, rather than flourish to see the possibility of living other kinds of lives. This was the reason Lorde claimed throughout her life the many identities that mattered for her with such relish and authority. She refused being denied the breadth and range of humanity that was her birthright as a member not of the black but of the human race.

For Lorde, for one to avoid being stunted it was necessary for society to become genuinely and thoroughly egalitarian. This egalitarianism had to work on two levels—within ourselves and within our society. Lorde often made a point of describing herself with all the adjectives she felt appropriate for her desires and aspirations: a black, lesbian, feminist, socialist, poet, mother of two, and partner in an interracial domestic arrangement. In her essay "There Is No Hierarchy of Oppression," Lorde again deftly moved between layers of address. She signaled that a main problem of her life was that any one of the identities she claimed for herself would likely be seen by the dominant group—read here, white heterosexuals, especially men—as deviant. This posed a problem, since it would compel anyone in a similar situation to align with the least contested identity. But the beauty of Lorde's thought and writing is her attentiveness to self-care in the name of social justice: "I simply do not believe that one aspect of myself can possibly profit from the oppression of any other part of my identity."[19]

This is not all that was exceptional about Lorde. Indeed, her commitment to social justice with respect to sensual autonomy as well as racial politics distinguished her among black thinkers of her time. The main theme in all her work was the relationship between full possession of oneself and the power this should provide each of us in having an effective say in our society's political, economic, and social arrangements.[20] Personal authority itself depended, of course, on the absence of abject oppression. It also depended on one's courage to reach deep within oneself and outwardly express the urgency of the forms of human community one needed to feel whole and fulfilled. Among the wells of power within each of us, Lorde was keen to highlight erotic power. To get a sense of her philosophical commitment to this position, consider the following claims: first, "The erotic is a resource within each of us . . . firmly rooted in the power of our unexpressed or unrecognized feeling. In order to perpetuate itself, every oppression must corrupt or distort those various sources of power within the culture of the oppressed that can provide energy for change."[21] Thus, oppression affects not only formal rights and laws or the psychology of planning and hoping, but also intimate identification, which Lorde insists is one source of social and political power. "This is one reason the erotic is so feared, and so often relegated to the bedroom alone, when it is recognized at all. For once we begin to feel deeply all the aspects of our lives, we begin to demand from ourselves and from our life-pursuits that they feel in accordance with that joy which we know ourselves to be capable of."[22] The special place of the erotic in our lives, then, is to more tightly bind us to the ideas of fulfillment and appreciation. In being attuned with that which fulfills us we have one more tool at our disposal with which to observe and criticize our social circumstances.

The attention to sensuality and the erotic proved an effective analytic category in Lorde's hands. She saw at least two threats to erotic awareness and, thereby, the possibilities of resistance to oppression. One, of course, was the problem of sexism and sexual violence perpetrated by men, white and black. The other is possibly unexpected. We must remember that despite our popular images of sexual liberation in the 1960s and among the Woodstock generation, philosophical engagement with sex and pornography were not as prevalent as they are today. In one of her most outstanding interviews, Lorde spoke on the theme of sadomasochism in the gay community with Susan Leigh Star. The purpose of their exchange was to make some political sense of S/M practices. One very powerful view Lorde staked out was that S/M is a way for capitalist society to commodify the "deviant" yet alluring sexual practices of homosexuals. On the one hand, homophobia and discrimination against those who embrace a queer lifestyle were rampant. Thus members of the LGBT community could not count on various kinds of basic fairness in American society. Yet, on the other hand, the market seemed to highly value spectacles of LGBT sexuality that centered on intimate violence or acts that implied violence and oppression. This should strike us as true both in Lorde's time and in our own. It raises what seems to me an even deeper question for Lorde that has to do, again, with the distribution of power. "Sadomasochism feeds the belief that domination is inevitable and legitimately enjoyable."[23] This tendency to intimately prize domination under the auspices of a capitalist society that also regularly practices oppression emphasized for Lorde the role of self-care—"I'm not questioning anyone's right to live. I'm saying we must observe the implications of our lives. If what we are talking about is feminism, then the personal is political and we can subject everything in our lives to scrutiny. We have been nurtured in a sick, abnormal society, and we should be about the process of reclaiming ourselves as well as the terms of that society."[24]

Liberation thereby becomes a matter of our inner lives being sufficiently unshackled from the invasion of dominant expectations and manipulations of market-driven fetishes to meet the requirements of living freely in a democratic society marked by respect and openness.

In this way, Lorde, like Cooper, anticipated the "all lives matter" retort to "black lives matter" but developed a response from a different angle. Where Cooper's anticipatory response centered on the idea of equal humanity, and thus the centrality of black women, Lorde seems to aim a bit more squarely at the ideology of dominance. She wrote, "The increasing attacks upon lesbians and gay men are only an introduction to the increasing attacks upon all Black people, for wherever oppression manifests itself in this country, Black people are potential victims."[25] The need to support homosexuals is predicated not on the particularity of the struggle for gay rights but on the logic of group domination coupled with the deeper history of black Americans' experiences with the logic of oppression. For Lorde, blacks who did not support gay rights, especially those of black gays and lesbians, failed to see that the struggle of homosexuals was not of a different kind from their own, but, rather, was simply taking place in another key. At issue is the freedom of bodies and the liberty of the souls and minds in those bodies. In both cases, black lives matter not in the particularity of the lifestyles straight or gay blacks expressed but, rather, in the generality of the irrational reasons given for suppressing rights of blacks, straight or gay. Those motivated to oppress assume there is a "normal" way to live a life and that there is a "civilized" color that best embodies that normal way of life. Indeed, Lorde should in part be read as providing an extraordinarily robust response to historical white supremacy, because in all cases, black domination across the board was underwritten by the presumption that white masculinity was the barometer for normalcy and democratic acceptance. This contribution by Lorde remains not only powerful but exceptionally insightful. Though the killings of black Americans by citizens and the police have gotten more attention than ever in American history, due in part to the widespread availability of recording technology as well as easy access to the ubiquitous social media and alternative news outlets, coverage has dominantly centered on violence done to black men. A few cases involving black women have penetrated the public conversation, but this is not enough. In 2015, more than a dozen transgender black Americans were killed under questionable circumstances, and not one case got national attention. For Lorde, the tragedy here is twofold: that we do not know about these losses of life and that, as Americans, we don't seem to think those lives matter enough to be worth knowing about. All lives matter, indeed.

"When we deploy 'All Lives Matter' as to correct an intervention specifically created to address anti-blackness, we lose the ways in which the state apparatus has built a program of genocide and repression mostly on the backs of Black people—beginning with the theft of millions of people for free labor—and then adapted it to control, murder, and profit off of other communities of color and immigrant communities."[26] This is a statement made by Alicia Garza in a 2014 essay for the news and opinion outlet *The Feminist Wire*. It is sweeping in its scope and moral ambition. The equality it demands extends deep into the reaches of our economic vices, our preoccupation with law and order despite the state violence it begets, and the questionable legitimacy of some state institutions altogether. But Garza gave the piece a gendered title that played on the name of a supposedly neutral discipline—she dubbed the piece a "herstory" rather than a history. Why?

Well, for one thing, Garza, as a founder of BlackLivesMatter.org, sought to assert narrative authority over a story she has helped write and that is consistently under threat of being redirected or misused. But this is not the only issue at stake in Garza's insistence that her story be a "herstory." Garza stands in for a wide range of disaffected Americans, among them black women, and black Americans in the LGBT community, whose oppression can be just as murderous as that suffered by black straight men, but in so many ways more diffuse and ever present. Black women, for example, whose history in America has oscillated between being sexual predators of white women's husbands to being "mammies" to white families' children—between danger and source of security and nurturing—have been overlooked as being people with aspirations, hopes, fears, plans, desires, defeats, triumphs, and strength. The Black Lives Matter movement is trying to do more than correct for a deep history over the course of which blacks generally have been oppressed. Additionally, and importantly, the movement is also trying to morally and practically redirect a present-day social regime in which blackness is not only oppressed as a category but is also used to obscure the myriad disadvantages blackness enhances, augments, makes more severe. These are the depredations suffered by a wider community of blacks outside that of black men.

Eleanor Bumpurs would have benefited from a society more sensitive to this farther-reaching program of a progressive, radical black politics, as Sandra Bland would have. Each woman had a story leading to the moment our society snatched them away. Having suffered from poverty, gender oppression, and, apparently, the travails of mental illness, both women, and so many more, have been effectively erased from the frame of our democratic concern. Anna Julia Cooper and Audre Lorde were predecessors, even instructors, to those like Garza who think history is not enough. The desire to redeem, save, protect our sons, daughters, and all affected souls depends on our listening, valuing, laughing, crying, despairing and hoping over our shared herstory of black lives needing to matter.

WHERE IS THE LOVE? THE HOPE

FOR AMERICA'S REDEMPTION

> *If we are wrong, justice is a lie, love has no meaning. And we are determined here in Montgomery to work and fight until justice runs down like water, and righteousness like a mighty stream.*
>
> —MARTIN LUTHER KING JR., *address at Holt Street Baptist Church, 1955*

> *Love takes off the masks that we fear we cannot live without and we cannot live within. I use the word "love" here not merely in the personal sense but as a state of being, or a state of grace—not in the infantile American sense of being made happy but in the tough and universal sense of quest and daring and growth.*
>
> —JAMES BALDWIN, *The Fire Next Time*

"I ACKNOWLEDGE THAT I AM VERY angry," said the sister of DePayne Middleton-Doctor. "But one thing that DePayne always enjoined in our family . . . is she taught me that we are the family that love built. We have no room for hating, so we have to forgive. I pray God on your soul."[1]

At 8:59 p.m. on June 17, 2015, congregants were inside the Emmanuel African Methodist Episcopal Church in Charleston, South Carolina. It is one of the oldest AME churches in America, built in 1891, and has long served the local southern black community as a place of sanctuary, peace, and tolerance. At 9:01 p.m., the scene changed from humble worship to chaotic carnage. At 9:00 p.m., Dylann Storm Roof, a self-proclaimed white supremacist with ties to at least one hate group website, The Last Rhodesian, had single-handedly stormed the church. He opened fire, killing eight black Americans on the scene; one more victim died on the way to the hospital.

Roof was captured the next day, and an all-too-familiar scene began to play out. A perpetrator of racial hate was brought face-to-face with those he had irrevocably harmed, having stolen the lives of their loved ones, and the ones left picking up the pieces were faced with a choice. With the collective eyes of their friends and families, the officer of the court, and the nation on them, would they express the contempt Roof deserved or would they do something widely expected of blacks? Would they forgive the white supremacist terrorist who had summarily executed nine innocent black parishioners simply because he thought their lives didn't matter?

All who spoke in court chose to forgive Dylann Roof. One by one, they stood in public and extended forgiveness to a man who had murdered their friends and family in cold blood. Ms. Middleton-Doctor's sister's statement is especially extraordinary. She began where she ought, in voicing her own very justified feelings about the matter, which in this case was anger. She then invoked the memory of the one she had lost and honored the ethos that love built the family. She then pointed out that there is no room for hate, followed by the most crucial move of all: "so we have to forgive you." Is this relationship between love and mourning, between love and forgiveness, the right one? Did Ms. Middleton-Doctor's kin have to forgive Dylann Roof just because they had built their family on love? In forgiving Roof, what did she accomplish, and who was redeemed? And, importantly, what happens with the anger we acknowledge in ourselves after we have been grievously wronged time and time again? In what follows we engage two of the most powerful black writers on love to explore the role love ought to play in the lives of black Americans as they continue to exist under the sky of racial injustice.

James Baldwin and Martin Luther King Jr. were powerful proponents of the role of love in American race relations. For them, love was the key to democratic redemption. Baldwin and King urged Americans, past and present, near and far, you and I, to take seriously the importance of love in achieving a stable and lasting racial equality. For Baldwin, this love amounted to a willingness to reveal one's own vulnerabilities and to treat others' vulnerabilities with kindness and a large heart; it also meant putting justified resentment on hold in order to leave open the possibility for forgiveness—thus leaving open the possibility for healing. King had a slightly different view of love's importance. Though his ideas were rooted in Christian theology, King persistently advocated, in secular words and worldly action, a kind of love that would persuade one's enemies to see the injustice of their thoughts and actions by being unconditional even in the face of terrifying conditions. King's preference for disinterested love, what the ancient Greeks called *agape*, held in esteem the virtues of an evildoer's humanity while condemning the evil he committed. This left open the possibility of acceptance in the form of genuine human community. For each of them, love was the means to forgiveness and acceptance, while redemption was the means to securing not only blacks' rights and liberties but their mortal safety. For Baldwin and King laws without love could only ever amount to a tacit acknowledgment that black lives were acknowledged but not that they ultimately mattered.

By 1965, James Baldwin had left and returned to America in search of an answer to the question all black Americans inevitably asked themselves during the dark years of Jim Crow: how might I find my place among equals despite my race? American racism, as well as homophobia, had provoked in him a deep disdain for the white cruelty, fear, and loathing toward blacks that had become so deeply ingrained in American life. It is surprising, then, to hear Baldwin in a 1965 debate with American conservative William Buckley express a kind of affectionate possessiveness over white Americans. His sentiments suggest lovers who cannot stand to be together but who also cannot bear being apart. Baldwin says:

> What I always felt when I finally left the country, found myself abroad and other places, and watched the Americans abroad—and these are my countrymen, and I do care about them, and even if I didn't there is something between us, we have the same shorthand. I know, when I look at a girl or boy from Tennessee, where they come from in Tennessee and what that means. No Englishman knows that, no Frenchman—no one in the world[!] knows that except another black man who comes from the same place. And one watches these lonely people denying the only kin they have.[2]

Baldwin expressed this view and sentiment to a room of white Europeans at the Cambridge Union in the United Kingdom. The debate between him and Buckley, both lively and ultimately heavily one-sided in Baldwin's favor, had taken up the question of whether the "American dream" had come at the expense of black Americans. This is an interesting and pressing question, to be sure. It is an easy guess to say that Baldwin felt the American dream did and does come at the expense of black Americans. Less immediately apparent is how Baldwin calculated that expense.

James Baldwin was born in 1924 in New York City to a single mother. His mother, Berdis Jones, eventually married David Baldwin, a New Orleans native whose mother had been a slave. James accepted David as his father. This placed James two generations away from slavery—not that Baldwin had an especially high regard for the quality of blacks' limited freedom in his day. Of course, most blacks at the time would have said that their condition in America was preferable to that in the first half of the nineteenth century or earlier. The death of slavery, however, did not spell the death of oppression or racial danger. In a peculiar way, blacks' social position became more treacherous. White Americans' great rush to point to a significant change, such as the Emancipation Proclamation, as having satisfied the demands of racial equality made it increasingly difficult to pinpoint the systemic causes of blacks' social, economic, and political woes. The persistence of lynching as well as Klan-perpetrated mob terror continued to provide at least one hook on which civil rights activists could hang their complaints. However, other than these clear abuses of human life, those pressing for racial equality needed modified statements of the sources of racial inequality to effectively make their case to an American public that was less than sympathetic. The average white American in the middle of the twentieth century did not grasp that "separate but equal" was a moral offense against blacks. Blacks saw deeper into that principle—they rightly perceived that separate meant quite the opposite of equal and that Jim Crow was white supremacy by any means necessary. And this tended to impact blacks' ability to place their humanity on a par with that of the white Americans passing through Harlem at their leisure, voting at the polls as was their liberty, and saving money to buy a nice house for the family from the proper wages they earned at the jobs that they had fair opportunities to obtain.

This American way of life that discounted black humanity preoccupied Baldwin all his years. The black body has always been at the center of racial inequality in America—how could it not, given our irrational preoccupation with skin color? But as America moved from Reconstruction to the Civil Rights Act, racial ire was directed through other forms of disadvantage and coercion, such as substandard segregated housing and ever-intensifying police repression. This left a young, precocious, and searching Baldwin in need of a means to make sense of a senseless society and find a place in an inhospitable nation. As with many in the black community, his first stop was the black church.

Baldwin spent a brief span of his mid-teenage years in the pulpit of the church attending to blacks' spirituality. His initiating encounter was at Mount Calvary of the Pentecostal Faith with Bishop Rosa Artemis Horn, who asked at that first meeting, "Whose little boy are you?" Baldwin's biographer recalls for us that "Baldwin was struck later by the fact that exactly that same question had been asked him by 'pimps and racketeers' who wanted him to 'hang out' with them."[3] With the lingering doubts about whether the church wasn't just one more hustle in an environment built on hustles, Baldwin concluded that his true calling was not in the church. Nevertheless, his spirituality is astounding and resonates clearly in the parts of his writing that seek to convey to readers what it costs blacks to be treated as less than human. For example, "I can conceive of no Negro native to this country who has not, by the age of puberty, been irreparably scarred by the conditions of his life. All over Harlem, Negro boys and girls are growing up into stunted maturity, trying desperately to find a place to stand, and the wonder is not that so many are ruined but that so many survived."[4] Baldwin does not speak about violence explicitly, yet he suggests the idea of survival. Freedom and rights aren't simply a matter of *not* being in slavery but of not being at the mercy of whites' contempt.

It is commonplace in the history of racial struggle to focus on the uses and necessity of rights. All Americans rely on this language to press political claims. It is therefore curious and compelling that the theme of rights plays so negligible a role in Baldwin's criticisms and exhortations. How is it that a man writing during the most tempestuous years of the civil rights movement could afford to pay scant attention to the central idea in that movement: rights? The answer is simpler than you might imagine and has to do with Baldwin's own brand of spirituality, with love being central to his thinking.

The basic truth about rights is that they are near useless for the oppressed so long as they live in a society that abandons, neglects, abuses, mortally threatens, cajoles, and holds them in contempt. On this point Baldwin was perspicuous. A democratic life is not merely one in which you are free to walk the streets or vote or own property. An important aspect of democratic life is being free to walk the streets among others who hold you in basic regard, to vote for candidates who are at least capable of acknowledging and taking seriously your needs, to own property in a community of peers in which the idea of friendship is genuinely possible. And these aspects of public democratic life mean a great deal for one's spiritual existence, for one's inner life. Baldwin saw clearly the deep importance of there being not only coherence but harmony between Americans' inner lives and their public lives. And Baldwin saw painfully that blacks' inner lives were constantly under threat of being ravaged by the apathy and callousness of American racism. This marks the deep significance of love for Baldwin. Black Americans cannot ultimately make their white counterparts into the people they wish they were, though they may do their best to compel them to be just in spirit as well as in law. But failing that, blacks must continue to get by day-to-day, and they owe it to themselves to not only tend to their suffering but to do what they can to enrich their self-conception, to safeguard their inner lives from the destructive force of racial hatred. As Baldwin said pitch perfectly: "Incontestably, alas, most people are not, in action, worth very much; and yet, every human being is an unprecedented miracle. One tries to treat them as the miracles they are, while trying to protect oneself from the disasters they've become."[5] What happens when one does not protect oneself from the disasters people have become? What happens to black Americans who do not protect themselves from the disasters known as racists? Their ire toward the white world for rejecting them begins to turn inward with devastating consequences, as Baldwin warns his nephew in *The Fire Next Time*.

The secular definition of "prophet" is a person with visionary insight into an issue, with that vision possibly reaching into the future. This leads to the common notion that prophets have the power to predict. Baldwin's self-description was typically that of witness—he felt strongly that bearing witness was the writer's true vocation. But *The Fire Next Time* is a gripping example of Baldwin's prophetic capacities as well. If you note the title, you will also guess the nature of Baldwin's prophecy—an America that fails to finally live up to its own ideals will only put in place the circumstances for its downfall. The darkness of the theme is all the more reason to appreciate Baldwin's frequent and urgent references to love, an idea that gets more usage in this work than in almost any other of his nonfiction. And it tellingly begins with a brief letter from Baldwin to his nephew.

Why does Baldwin begin an essay thematically concerned with the salvation of a nation with a letter to his nephew? Baldwin may have been playing, with particular verve, the role of the prophet in *The Fire Next Time*, but, if so, he sought to be a responsible prophet by building on those circumstances of American life to which he bore witness. Through the meeting of witness-bearing and prophecy Baldwin positioned himself to focus not merely on salvation but on redemption, and redemption comes through love. Baldwin loved his nephew deeply, and his opening letter, importantly titled, "My Dungeon Shook: Letter to My Nephew on the One Hundredth Anniversary of the Emancipation," sets the example for how you and I might come to terms with the emotional and spiritual difficulties of black life. The first lesson is contained in Baldwin's sardonic comment on the life and death of his own stepfather, a man with whom Baldwin had an intensely combative relationship. Baldwin writes to his nephew, "Well, [your grandfather] is dead, he never saw you, and he had a terrible life; he was defeated long before he died because, at the bottom of his heart, he really believed what white people said about him."[6] Baldwin's transition in such a short space from detached reportage to emotional and psychological insight makes this a moving passage. His succinct account initially strikes us as clinical and cold (Well, your grandfather is dead, he never saw you, and he had a terrible life) but Baldwin's apparent detachment is meant to set up an awful revelation—his father's spirit was extinguished not merely by white racism but also, crucially, by his own failure to love himself. Otherwise he would never have believed "at the bottom of his heart" the things white people thought and said about him, that they think and say about blacks.

During James's childhood, Baldwin's father found himself in just the sort of a predicament that tested his resilience against the effects of racism. James Baldwin's white elementary school teacher, Orilla Miller, took a great interest in him and developed an independent relationship with him that included taking the young James to see shows and movies. There was nothing salacious in the relationship. She had observed in James an uncommon intellectual probing and promise, and she wanted to protect and cultivate that capacity, knowing full well how delicately positioned black potential was in white-supremacist America. The nature of the predicament, then, was something different than the stuff of scandals. Rather, David Baldwin despised white Americans, yet he did not object to Orilla taking up a custodial role in his son's life. And this to James constituted both a mark of cowardice and self-betrayal on the part of his stepfather. On James's view, his father not only lacked the courage of his convictions but was intimidated by whites—"at the bottom of his heart he really believed what white people said about him"—and this resulted in James's being in a sense "turned over" to a white woman, his father's enemy. But we should not be confused by this. James sensed a kindred spirit in

Orilla; but he had also, by a young age, determined that white Americans were not his or his father's friends—and it was David Baldwin's cowing, when his protection mattered most to James, that left a lasting impression. This was a significant reason Baldwin lacked an abiding respect for his father. He felt that "Negroes in this country . . . are taught really to despise themselves from the moment their eyes open on the world."[7] Baldwin's failure to take more secure possession of his son was symptomatic in James's eyes of the self-loathing gnawing at his stepfather's inner life.

Baldwin's concern that self-love would ultimately be replaced by the tendency to despise oneself was, however, not only a reaction to his fathers' various failures. Baldwin similarly lamented many of his friends' inabilities during their teenage and young adult years to successfully face down the oppression their spirits underwent in the face of calamitous disadvantage. Baldwin spoke of these friends congregating in the hallways of apartment buildings, getting drunk and blaming "the man" for their defeat; "and there seemed to be no way whatever to remove this cloud that stood between them and the sun."[8] A similar sentiment marked what eventually developed into Baldwin's deep suspicion of the church. Speaking on the notion of heavenly compensation for Earthly woes that he was compelled to peddle during his teenage years in the pulpit, Baldwin wrote, "Were only Negroes to gain this crown? . . . Perhaps I might have been able to reconcile myself even to this if I had been able to believe there was any loving-kindness to be found in the haven I represented. . . . I really mean that there was no love in the church. It was a mask for hatred and self-hatred and despair."[9] In neither passage did Baldwin chastise his friends or congregation. Baldwin possessed a sensitive spirit, and he was aware that there were reasons people became crumpled and ugly. And even though his father's self-defeat did sting him, Baldwin understood that his father's inability to love others was crucially linked to his inability to love himself; both capacities to love had been tragically deadened.

Why does the idea that one cultivates a love of self and others in order to become a whole person, a person of integrity, a person with dignity, matter for politics? Democracy might require two—me and you—but if you insist on casting me out while holding the keys to the goods and benefits to which my humanity rightly entitles me, how do I get you to accept me? Baldwin's position is as elegant as it is burdened by our history. He felt that you have to come to love me. More trying for black Americans, he thought that a very good way, maybe the only good way of securing others' love was to love others first and well. He notified his nephew:

> Please try to remember that what they believe, as well as what they do and cause you to endure, does not testify to your inferiority but to their inhumanity and fear.... There is no reason for you to try to become like white people and there is no basis whatever for their impertinent assumption that *they* must accept *you*. The really terrible thing, old buddy, is that *you* must accept *them*. And I mean that very seriously. You must accept them and accept them with love. For these innocent people have no hope.[10]

Baldwin went on:

> And if the word *integration* means anything, this is what it means: that we, with love, shall force our brothers to see themselves as they are, to cease fleeing from reality and begin to change it.[11]

Baldwin first warned his nephew to avoid the path his own father took, which, as Baldwin described it, led to self-defeat. He then advised him to take a stout stance, to set his feet and understand how acceptance really ought to work in a racially troubled society like America's. If blacks are the ones being put upon and hounded and harassed, then it can only mean that it really is the prerogative of the hounded and harassed to choose to accept the hunters and harassers.

We have to appreciate Baldwin's attempt here to empower his nephew, and through him, us. Baldwin's counsel that blacks accept whites came with the condition that the acceptance can be neither grudging nor hesitant. While one ought not love irresponsibly, one should also not be said to love merely technically. Love requires an investment of mind but also of spirit. The investment of spirit here is clearly therapeutic. Racial oppression and abuse tends to motivate a person to turn the attention of the oppressed and the abused on herself, to grapple with the ways and means of living day-to-day in a society in which acceptance is both rare and insecure. This broadly leads to despair, and despair can subsequently manifest self-hatred and self-pity, two extremes of reactionary emotions and attitudes. But, as with Baldwin's father, this leads to defeat before one even dies. Loving another person is a powerful thing. When we truly love another we essentially affirm our own humanity. We put our vulnerability on the line by opening ourselves to others' virtues and vices. When we love, we form and affirm for ourselves the principles by which we intend on entering into partnerships. When we love, we often invite others to examine their own vulnerability and seek to assure them that they are safe with us, that we will make everything okay. When we love, we set the standards by which the other party must abide for our love to be ongoing. Most powerfully, when we love, we transform from victims into persons of honor and dignity; we transform from the downtrodden to the authors of our lives. But not only this. When we love, we invite others to take responsibility for what they think, say, and do—we empower them to realize that they can be better people, that character is malleable when the will to face the challenge of love rises to the occasion. If and when all this can be done, love leads to our collective redemption. We realize and reconcile ourselves to the fact that we, each of us, are humans with not only equal capacities but equal needs. Love delivers what democracy promises: equality and fairness.

In 1964, the year the Civil Rights Act was signed into law, Harlem was shaken by a scene with which we are today familiar. On April 17 of that year, a group of children turned over a local vendor's fruit stand. This was mischievous, to be sure, but what happened next with the police was out of proportion with the crime. It began when one man, Frank Stafford, placed himself between the children and the police, who had cornered and begun beating the children. He asked if the beating was necessary. What followed is a tale as macabre as it is tragically believable. The police, resenting the challenge, turned their ire on Stafford, beating him in the street, beating him in the precinct after his arrest, and taking him to the hospital to get him cleared as "healthy," only to then beat him more back in the precinct—a not uncommon regimen of off-the-books corporal punishment at the time. Stafford paid for his question with an eyeball. Stafford had been so badly beaten in the face that his eye was damaged beyond repair and had to be removed. He endured the aftermath of this abuse, while the responsible police officers eluded penalties for their own crimes. Even worse, though Stafford didn't die, his patch marked him as a constant target for police harassment whenever he was on the street, as he had become known among the precinct officers as a black man who did not "know his place."

Baldwin's emphasis on love was not the result of an idealist's willful ignorance of the tough circumstances on America's streets. He had written on Stafford's abuse. It was on account of his bearing witness that Baldwin harbored resentment toward white Americans' instruments of power, especially the police. For example:

> Now what I have said about Harlem is true . . . of every Northern city with a large Negro population. And the police are simply the hired enemies of this population. They are present to keep the Negro in his place and to protect white business interests, and they have no other function. They are, moreover—even in a country which makes the grave error of equating ignorance with simplicity—quite stunningly ignorant; and since they know that they are hated, they are always afraid. One cannot possibly arrive at a more sure-fire formula for cruelty.
>
> This is why those pious calls to "respect the law," always to be heard from prominent citizens each time the ghetto explodes, are so obscene. The law is meant to be my servant and not my master, still less my torturer and murderer. To respect the law, in the context in which the American Negro finds himself, is simply to surrender his self-respect.[12]

This searing indictment expresses and harbors resentment toward white Americans' instruments of power. It does not signal that Baldwin thought the difference between whites and the instruments at their disposal were always distinct. Indeed, most of the police officers at the time of Baldwin's

"Report from Occupied Territory" were white, so there's that. However, notice the features that seem to promote (at least some) police misconduct: ignorance, improper usage of a tool in the name of police protecting business interests instead of the law proper, and the police's awareness of being hated by blacks. Baldwin shrewdly avoided the easier categorical indictment of whites and instead indicted poor judgment and a bad relationship, based on the police force's historical abuse of blacks. But Baldwin kept all the constituencies that made up his readership at the table of his writing and message. It is easy to read this as an invitation to blacks to not respect the law or to riot or react violently. But seeing things this way would be to go one step too far, too fast. By "respect" Baldwin really meant "respect"—blacks who must endure such conditions do not owe the law their positive esteem. And that is all. To esteem the law which abuses you is to lack respect for yourself as the abused.

Blacks, then, face a very tangible predicament. Baldwin's call for blacks to love themselves is demanding, but his additional call for blacks to love whites despite the pains and torments of racial oppression can sometimes seem unreasonably demanding. It calls to mind a kind of schizophrenia in which my self-respect requires anger against white power but in which my soul also requires that I be compassionate *despite* the rage. Baldwin was a witness, and may have been a prophet, but he was no hypocrite: "I knew the tension in me between love and power, between pain and rage, and the curious, the grinding way, I remained extended between these two poles—perpetually attempting to choose the better rather than the worse. But this choice was in terms of a personal, a private better[.]"[13] Baldwin's career was consumed with affirming the worth, the sanctity of black life—he saw it as his vocation to make Americans aware that black life mattered and that racism was destroying that life in the deepest sense—blacks' humanity was under constant threat, and the fire next time would come at the point at which even Baldwin himself would concede that loving the person who benefits from your pain is a fool's errand. However, despair is the vice of the weak. Baldwin knew that persevering until a more just society could be secured was a taxing spiritual demand. Despite these doubts, he took seriously the charge of being a witness as well as the ambition to be sympathetic. This meant that how people act made a difference to Baldwin; but he didn't think that was the whole story. Human action is always shaped by the private space of our imaginations, hopes, and fears: "Though we do not believe it yet, the interior life is a real life, and the intangible dreams of people have a tangible effect on the world."[14] Love is the best the interior life has to offer others and, importantly, ourselves, for it conditions and holds hopes and fears in their proper places while urging us to put to good use our capacity to accept others and temper the tendency to be judgmental.

It is doubtful Baldwin felt he had secured the love of white Americans by the time he died of cancer in 1987. The success of his career establishes that his skills were esteemed, but we have learned from him already that the esteem of a person's qualities apart from the person who possesses those qualities is an empty and vacuous infatuation—as fickle as it is glamorous. The question of whether Baldwin had secured genuine love is additionally hampered by the fact that his investigation of a large number of murders in Atlanta, Georgia, had concluded and been published just two years before his death. Given the cynicism and bitterness Baldwin expressed in that work, it would be cavalier to mistake our own admiration of his intellectual prowess and largeness of spirit for white America's love for the man. To do so would be to trivialize his reportage's final attempt to alert Americans to the moral and democratic disaster they court in continuing to deny that black lives matter. Indeed, it is tragically ironic that one of Baldwin's last major works concerned a gruesome series of murders involving black youth. Baldwin not only thought that the murders had been investigated poorly but also found it tragically ironic that a black man was pursued for the crimes for reasons that were spurious but familiar to anyone with some knowledge of the ways blacks are easily cast as villains. This tragic irony—Baldwin's final years investigating black death—holds one final lesson for us. In what is referred to as "The Last Interview" two years after *The Evidence of Things Not Seen* was published, Quincy Troupe asked Baldwin how he had tried to deal with his growing notoriety early in his career. Baldwin claimed to have felt trapped, and Troupe asked him what he thought he had been before he was trapped. Baldwin responded thusly, "I was a witness, I thought."—and this is really all Baldwin wanted to be. He did not seek to be a personality or public figure. Both kinds of status always threaten to distract others and oneself from the reasons anyone should be paying attention and taking a person's ideas seriously.[15] In Baldwin's words one again senses the importance of the witness called to pay attention to the state of our society and to be brave enough to remark on it, criticize it, as well as possess the faith that bearing witness can lead to a better day.

Every savior needs a witness, and James Baldwin would be that person on March 24, 1965. Martin Luther King Jr. "stood on the flood-lit platform with his pant-legs rolled up over knee-length hiking boots, and he led the crowd in the movement's ritual chant."[16] When King shouted, "What do you want!" Baldwin was among the thousands who shouted back, "Freedom!" When King wanted to know when the demand needed to be met by asking, "When do you want it?" it is a sure thing Baldwin responded, "Now!" without hesitation, as did the thousands of other black Americans desperate for the rights they were owed. For Baldwin, King personified the tension between resisting white power and embracing white Americans that marked his own inner struggle, as we saw above. In King, Baldwin recognized a brother in the essential struggle for his own and others' humanity and for whom the power of love was a power for redemption and change: "[T]he fact that King really loves the people he represents and has—*therefore*—no hidden, interior need to hate the white people who oppose him has had and will, I think, continue to have the most far-reaching and unpredictable repercussions on our racial situation."[17] Baldwin was there to witness a man, who would become one of history's great social movement leaders, inspire all in attendance to tolerate the mud that surrounded them that day on the soggy outdoor field—a mud so deep and inconvenient that it hindered the government agents who were scouring the field for bombs to keep the gathered activists and protesters safe from the kind of racist retribution that had been visited on black churches throughout the South. The next day King would lead close to twenty-five thousand people on the final leg of the historic march from Selma, Alabama, to Montgomery, Alabama, in the effort to secure blacks' voting rights.

One year earlier, King claimed a major victory for the cause of racial justice in helping ensure that the Civil Rights Act was signed into law July 2, 1964. No event as momentous as this can be traced to one single cause or person. But both sensitive minds and history agree on one point: the day when blacks attained formal equality would not have been possible *without* Martin Luther King Jr., or at least not by 1964. And the August day in 1965 when blacks secured the vote would not have been possible *without* King leading the chant that demanded freedom now. What was it about King that made his presence so crucial? A great deal has been made of King's commitment to nonviolence. Most Americans can cite the marches and protests he helped organize or his willingness to go to jail without resisting arrest. In the popular mind, though, the focus on nonviolence has preempted the appreciation of the thinking behind King's powerful strategy.

Despite his father's misgivings, King attended the left-leaning, dominantly white Crozer Theological Seminary, beginning in the fall of 1948. His years there were formative in more ways than one. While studying at Crozer he developed a robust repertoire of philosophical interlocutors from the history of Western thought—Plato, Augustine, Georg Hegel, and Immanuel Kant—as well as from the theological canon—Reinhold Niebuhr, Walter Rauschenbusch, and Paul Tillich—and he would continuously impress his audiences on the occasions when he chose to explicitly invoke his intellectual influences. But he also experienced other, maybe less fortunate opportunities for growth. Despite its intellectual liberalism, not all the students at Crozer were enamored with the idea of racial egalitarianism, and this would at times cause tensions. However, King was already in possession of the basic principle that would define his legacy. As the notable King scholar Taylor Branch remarked, "King expressed the belief that love and reason could bring out in all people a basic goodness that was deeper than racial hatred or personal animosities."[18]

Whereas Baldwin viewed love as a personal virtue that centered on the willingness to be personally vulnerable, King's conception of the kind of love that mattered for racial equality—while broad and embracing—might strike one as a bit impersonal. For King, love was also a virtue, but its source and purposes were different. The virtue of love for King was, as Branch observed, tightly coupled with deliberative reasoning; one committed to love and then figured out how love mattered to the ethical question of the moment. One then endeavored to persuade an audience to moral rightness because one loved them. The target of the kind of love King endorsed was not the space of interpersonal intimacy but the mechanics and landscape of democratic co-participation. How does this work?

In early 1963, Kenneth Clark—the child psychologist who demonstrated with dolls that black children often develop a diminished sense of their own beauty and worth on account of racist standards of beauty—interviewed King and was especially interested in the logic behind the practice of nonviolence. King made two especially notable remarks. First:

> Now, the love ethic is another dimension which goes into the realm of accepting nonviolence as a way of life. There are many people who will accept nonviolence as the most practical technique to be used in a social situation, but they would not go to the point of seeing the necessity of accepting nonviolence as a way of life.[19]

Second: "I'm not talking about friendship. I find it pretty difficult to like people like Bull Connor . . . but I think you can love where you can't like the person because life is an affectionate quality."[20]

A deep issue in political life has to do with the nature of the agreements we make and the basis on which they are made. Within the field of political philosophy, for example, there is a distinction between what is called a *modus operandi* and a *modus vivendi*. We can refer to these respectively as a way of cooperating and a way of living, and this is the kind of important distinction King was making. When we approach complex and contentious issues, we are always asking or preparing to ask for a sacrifice of some sort. If I am part of a group pressing for an increase in the minimum wage, I am effectively asking a corporation to sacrifice profits. When I debate with my friends or co-workers the justice of more lenient sentencing laws, I am asking them to sacrifice what they take to be a sense of safety. Whether there are good moral reasons for a stance on either side of these and other issues, there is no getting around the fact that people and institutions often have to give up something they take to be important in order to meet even justified demands. Similarly, our demands are always made against the backdrop of democratic politics— what we ask for must ultimately be *given* and that almost never happens without something being *taken*, so those of us making demands must also be prepared to give; this is the nature of civic compromise that separates democracy from totalitarianism. This is the kind of trade the doctrine of nonviolence requires—you demand political goods, in this case, rights—and you must give up your sense of the entitlement to rage and retaliation, even when you are met with resentment and a billy club to the knees or a brick to the head.

You don't have to be a political philosopher or seasoned grassroots activist to see that in the case of black civil rights in the middle of the twentieth century, this trade was awful for those making the demands, and it was corrupted by those who refused to meet the demands. King and others in the nonviolent tradition of civil protest understood what was being asked of movement activists who sat at lunch counters not lifting a finger as whites cursed and spat at "the niggers" making trouble. It was the very terrible personal sacrifice and great courage demanded by that moment that moved King to discourage others from thinking of nonviolence as a merely instrumental strategy. He, rather, wanted nonviolence to be seen as a distinct and enduring ethos. If you were to place yourself at that lunch counter thinking nonviolence was a smart strategy, only to be smacked and spat upon, well, what would stop you from thinking the next day that maybe what you really needed was a gun to show people you mean business? Today's clever idea can always replace yesterday's bad strategy. And this is exactly why King pressed nonviolence as a way of life rather than as a way of cooperating.

But what has nonviolence to do with love? King knew that his position within the black community was situated between the opposite ends of the spectrum of blacks' attitudes about agitating for change. At one end were blacks who didn't want trouble and were not interested in fighting the contentious and dangerous fight for social justice because they were too preoccupied on a daily basis with making ends meet. On the other end were more militant black organizations and leaders, including Malcolm X, who publicly and scorchingly accused King's nonviolence doctrine of mimicking Uncle Tom blackness. As Malcolm X famously said, "It's time to stop singing and start swinging." Here, the reference to singing has to do with those slaves who, "fortunate" enough to work in the master's house, would spend time singing, often at the master's instruction or just to pass the time—these slaves came to be referred to as "House Niggas" or "Uncle Toms." Malcolm X's aggressive slogan called black Americans to wake up, stop thinking they had it good just because they weren't in the fields, and start fighting. Malcolm felt that nonviolence looked uncomfortably like cowardice. But King stood firm in the conviction that Malcolm and those who agreed with him didn't really understand how radical nonviolence was. As he once put it, "It must be emphasized that nonviolent resistance is not a method for cowards; it does resist. If one uses this method because he is afraid or merely because he lacks the instruments of violence, he is not truly nonviolent. . . . This is ultimately the way of the strong man."[21] So King thought a person didn't have to swing (or shoot or stab or bludgeon) to fight. Instead, nonviolence is a means to winning two fights. The first is internal—not unlike Baldwin's concern with one's internal life—and has to do with what King referred to as "internal violence of the spirit."[22] Once we overcome internal violence we are positioned to put to work King's conception of love toward others. This outward-facing love was both demanding and kind: it demanded the fundamental respect all persons are owed and, in return, offered it with humility.

King received his doctorate in theological philosophy, in 1955, from Boston University. In reading his works one quickly understands that he was as much an academic as he was a preacher or activist. For example, he had a deep understanding of ancient Greek thought and followed the ancients in their tripartite conception of love. Today, we tend to think of love as more or less one kind of emotional attitude, grounded in intimate affection and commitment that can manifest itself as close friendship or as romantic engagement. The ancient Greeks, in contrast, had a more systematic view. One conception of love for the ancients was *eros*—a love based in the passions—which we today understand as leading to lust, usually physical. Next came *philia*—this is love of persons, not erotically but also not disinterestedly. If you love your sibling, you are loving according to *philia*, for example. Finally came the form of love that underwrote King's doctrine of nonviolence, *agape*. King clarified for us:

> *Agape* does not begin by discriminating between worthy and unworthy people, or any qualities people possess. It begins by loving others *for their sakes*. It is an entirely "neighbor-regarding-concern for others," which discovers the neighbor in every man it meets.[23]

Baldwin approached love of others as a kind of mutual vulnerability, so that love could be interested in the way *philial* love presses us to love kin. King's approach is tidier but more abstract in a manner familiar to professional and academic philosophers. King took seriously the method of professional philosophers in trying to isolate moral ideals, the merits of which could be appreciated through pure rational reflection; the kind of reflection that does not depend on input from experience. This is not to say King did not use the experiences of racial injustice in his thinking. Rather, he seemed to hold in equally high esteem this additional mode of ethical thinking. And here is another point worth noting: Baldwin's thinking was tightly tethered to his biography and reporting, thus more immediate and less systematic; while King's thinking was of course motivated by the problems he faced and observed in America, it was also tempered and structured by his academic training and propensities, lending his writing and thinking on love a far more cerebral quality. Let's see if we can make sense of it.

King said that he could dislike Bull Connor but nonetheless love him; he also said that *agape* love is love of others for their sakes. How are the two views compatible? I believe it has something to do with where King located the key issue. We have to follow him a bit down the theological philosopher's road. Two distinctions mattered to King—the difference between a sin and the sinner and the difference between racial conflict and moral conflict. King thought it was possible to disapprove of and fight the sin. If a person turns a fire hose on you, that is evil. In a move, however, that rankled leaders like Malcolm X, King, alongside Baldwin, thought that the very great tragedy of American racism was that it was tragically destroying and warping the characters of white persons, that it corrupted their moral sensibilities to an extent that their racist tendencies, even if relatively benign, affected their other beliefs, such as which kinds of policies were fit for a modern liberal democracy. Neither King nor Malcolm denied that blacks were paying a horrible and heavy price, but whereas Malcolm often felt that the person who turned the hose on you left himself open to equal retribution in light of his evil act, King felt that person had been himself "victimized by evil" and thus was owed an opportunity to be engaged as a moral equal and persuaded to the cause of social justice.[24]

Maybe even more galling to leaders like Malcolm X, King thought "the struggle in the South is not so much the tension between white people and Negro People. The struggle is rather between justice and injustice."[25] Here King came uncomfortably close to setting aside race as central to the struggle for justice, but anyone who thinks he goes all the way to letting white Americans off the hook would be overlooking one very important feature of his approach. For King, the end-game, as it were, was always redemption, and this is how love underwrites nonviolence. Earlier, I said that if we take nonviolence to just be a way of cooperating, my refusal to bring a weapon to a protest today can just as easily be reversed if you spit on me, thereby providing me a reason to believe that I have been foolish to not arm myself. So tomorrow I will bring my gun. But nonviolence as a way of life guided by love in King's sense looks beyond today and tomorrow. Its goal, in a very Christian-inspired secular sense, is to put into place a community of persons who can be characterized by peace and acceptance rather than strife and difference. In that society, race wouldn't have a place in determining the relationship among people—men and women would relate to each other just that way: as humans with needs and the capacity to meet others' needs. King always insisted that nonviolence was a means of persuading those who would not otherwise hear you. Being politically astute as well as a student of the ancient Greeks, he also knew that rhetoric is a key part of persuasion. Thus, when King said that the fight is between justice and injustice rather than between blacks and whites in the South, he was trying to get us to imagine a vision of the future to displace the dystopia of our present. On his view, the future should be defined by the idea of community and the neighbors who make communities gracious sites for mutual flourishing. On his view, the future should leave no place for the distinction and tension of friends versus enemies. To get us to love each other in the future, King sought to get us to morally imagine how we can love each other now.

***

The claim that black lives matter, we should have realized by now, is not only a claim about fairness under the law, the cessation of police brutality, the elimination of vigilantes and all other manner of mortal threats to black lives. For Baldwin and King, that claim should mean those things, of course, but also much more. Saying that black lives matter is a claim on the sentiments and sensibilities of all Americans. It represents the hope that if we bear witness, and bear it truly, we can see how important it is that we love each other and ourselves. We see that without this love, the fight for justice is stifled by compassion's defeat. We understand that the possibility for redemption will run up against the greater likelihood of complacency and the persistence of spiritual and political corruption. Without love, any attempt to achieve either community or the friendship on which community depends will likely fail.

This brings us back to the example that set up our reading of James Baldwin and Martin Luther King Jr. Dylann Storm Roof walked into one of the oldest southern black churches and with wanton hatred erased nine black lives as if they did not matter. Despite the rage this act would justifiably evoke from distant bystanders, much less the loved ones of those senselessly slain, the exact opposite was expressed to Roof in court. He was forgiven by all who spoke. Ms. Middleton-Doctor's sister explicitly stated that she was required to forgive, because her sister had counseled her into a life defined by love. One might think that the forgiver in this instance mortgaged her right to hold Roof accountable with the fury to which she was entitled. But this was not the case. Her very first words were "I acknowledge my anger." In doing so before extending forgiveness, Depayne's sister paid homage to her own feelings of hurt and rage. She also put all those bearing witness on notice that she was aware of the ways in which Dylann Roof had violated her, her sister, the other victims, and the church. She foregrounded her anger to notify all those who would hear her that her forgiveness was offered in light of her anger, not despite it; her forgiveness was informed by her insistence that she embrace her own humanity as well as persuade others to embrace reason and sympathy, rather than irrationality and hatred. Depayne's sister, in a deeply admirable manner, exemplified the ethos of Baldwin and King in her confrontation with Roof. She understood that our collective redemption hinges on not only the words we utter but the sentiments we express as the groundwork for justice.

As Baldwin expressed in *The Fire Next Time*, a work of both prophecy and witness, "The universe, which is not merely the stars and the moon and the planets, flowers, grass, and trees, but *other people*, has evolved no terms for your existence, has made no room for you, and if love will not swing wide the gates, no other power will or can."[26] If *we* are to prevent the fire next time, we must ask ourselves, where is the love?

THE RADICAL LESSONS WE HAVE

NOT YET LEARNED

African Americans . . . are living in hell.

—DONALD TRUMP, *Presidential debate*

I, too, am America.

—LANGSTON HUGHES, *"I, Too"*

THERE DOESN'T EXIST, THERE NEVER has existed, nor is there ever likely to exist something as monolithic, analytically neat, or presumptively coherent as "black identity." Black Americans are just as free and capable of disputing the details of their social and political existence as any other demographic group. Yet, we often use terms like "black politics" to signify what is supposed to be a more or less agreed upon social, economic, and political agenda to benefit those who are, by US standards, "racially" black. So there seems to be a serious discrepancy, since having a "black politics" seems to presume having a "black identity." This is not quite right. A "black politics" is not predicated so much on identity as on a shared condition among those who share the racial descriptor "black." And this shared condition is subject to either the actual or the very great likelihood of suffering significant inequality in America on account of being black. Blacks are certainly not the only ones susceptible to inequality and unfairness in America—as categorical inequalities, gender, sexual orientation, class, and disability remain serious obstacles to an egalitarian nation. Yet, blacks, with the exception of Native Americans, have suffered the widest, deepest, and, too frequently, the most murderous inequality for the longest stretch of our nation's history. Given our supposed commitment to life, liberty, and the pursuit of happiness, this kind of injustice is quite radical both in its intense focus and in its tragic outcomes. It is not common for us to think about inequality as radical, either in its effects or in its logic of targeting certain individuals for insidiously irrational reasons, such as skin color. Yet, racial inequality is just that—radical inequality. My proposal is that we meet it with a refreshed radical black politics in order to balance the scales of justice. Further, I propose that we take our initial cues for such a program from the very thinkers I have suggested gave us the foundations for the idea, "black lives matter."

Conceiving of a refreshed radical black politics faces serious obstacles. Some of these are local and private: basic failures of imagination, fear of what directly confronting power requires of each of us, or simple lack of motivation. Others are dispersed and public. In this latter category I am especially concerned with black public intellectuals guilty of what I call reverse *ressentiment*. In his provocative *The Genealogy of Morals*, the post–Romantic era German philosopher and philologist Friedrich Nietzsche accused Christians and Jews of *ressentiment*. Nietzsche thought that Christians' and Jews' inability to confront the hardness of the world compelled them to take up religions that celebrated weakness and forgiveness over the will to power and revenge. Nietzsche accused the adherents of these two religions of repackaging resentment as humility and calling it compassion, which for him was a great and cruel deceit. Nietzsche's beliefs about Western morals and religion are not our concern, but the mechanics of his accusations are surprisingly useful for our purposes.

A select group of conservative-minded race thinkers commonly argue that blacks have, in one form or another, become self-victimizing by refusing to take responsibility for a better racial future. These thinkers hold such views despite the fact that racial inequality has persisted as an institutional reality regardless of the merits of the Civil Rights Act of 1964. That law was indeed meant to usher in an era when racial striving would be on safe ground, and personal responsibility could mean what it is supposed to mean—exercising culpable agency under conditions that secure the sovereignty of one's judgment and civic capabilities. However, these conditions do not adequately exist for blacks in America today. Rather than fairly face what are admittedly increasingly amorphous and less explicit forms of racial offense (when blacks are not dying at the end of a police officer's gun, that is), black conservatives have turned their attention to those who already face the challenge of being black in America, and they have repackaged compassion as resentment and called it uplift. This is the reversal of sentiments under the guise of reasonability, the kind of deceit Nietzsche found so troubling as the twentieth century loomed on the horizon of modernity's political evolution.

The group of black conservative arguments I engage are not the main subject of this chapter. Rather, they are used as a Klaxon, alerting us to the need for a refreshed black radical politics. It might initially seem strange that rather than confronting white thinkers or white interests directly, I am choosing rather to confront conservative-minded blacks. My reasoning, however, is plain: conservative black intellectual-ism is essentially white liberalism gone terribly awry; it takes the promise of autonomy in a market-based democracy and transforms it into a fact. Then it moralizes that pseudo-fact to displace legitimate social and institutional blame. Thus, whatever I say to the smaller population of black conservative intellectuals should be taken by white liberals and conserva-tives, who more explicitly endorse this way of putting black life, as an intervention in the perverse notions of uplift to which so many wittingly and unwittingly subscribe. In these final pages, I bring together the intellectual contributions of our eight thinkers, synthesizing the key insights from each of the previous chapters to present a blueprint for the future of black politics that stands in opposition to the recommen-dations from those who do not comprehend the challenges of being black in America.

From Ida B. Wells and Frederick Douglass we learn the sociopolitical value of shame and the aspiration toward real freedom in America to help conceive of democratic reconfiguration. From Langston Hughes and Zora Neale Hurston we gain the democratic uses of civic imagination to mobilize competing re-presentations. Anna Julia Cooper and Audre Lorde are crucial in centering the importance of black women and queer identity in our politics to reap-proach the demands of self-care and self-possession. And from James Baldwin and Martin Luther King we get dis-tinct conceptions of love that nonetheless instruct us on developing compassion that is both intelligent and resis-tant. Our collection of thinkers present the case that there remain lessons to be learned in the coming years that will likely prove pivotal to whether America will ever be genu-inely racially just.

SHAMEFUL PUBLICITY

All societies, even indecent ones, are regulated by norms of acceptability. Indeed, it is often indecent societies that are most regulated by these kinds of norms. Norms of acceptability establish the kinds of behaviors, attitudes, and utterances to which one must adhere to display a "proper" attitude about one's community or society. For example, patriotism is a political stance that often embodies important norms of acceptability, such as an unqualified love for one's country; a deep, abiding affection for its traditions; and idealization of its ways of life. Patriotism is, in fact, a good example. That idea is frequently used to counter those who seek to undo the political policies and institutions that are the sources of marginalization and oppression.

In America, it is sometimes deemed uncivil, disloyal, or destabilizing to criticize laws and the agencies and agents that enforce laws. When unarmed blacks are killed by police officers, for example, and black Americans in return say harsh things against the police, it is often the case that those public speech acts come under fire for being un-American. Frederick Douglass and Ida B. Wells were marvelous patriots. Why? Because they sought to save America and make it stronger, yet knew the path to doing so would be uncomfortable for the privileged, who either held power or benefited from racially disparate structures of authority and influence.

There are two forms of destabilization activists and protesters can introduce into society. One form is structural—it denies the very form of government or institutions that wield power over the people. Many black nationalists, for example, have advised blacks to either leave or petition for a separate slice of American territory on the view that American democracy itself is irredeemable, illegitimately founded, and continuously hazardous to all but white Americans. Thus, they argue that blacks must denounce American democracy and act accordingly. Another form of destabilization is characterological. It affirms the idea and ideal of American democracy but openly recognizes that *as democracy is practiced*, very few of the benefits available to whites are freely or fairly available to blacks. This second form of destabilization is concerned with redemption by way of implication rather than exemption by way of denunciation. This second form of destabilization can be powerfully implemented by way of our first radical ethics—shameful publicity.

Shame is the moral emotion or sensibility we ought to feel when we realize our actions, beliefs, or attitudes in fact conflict with some prior held principle. If you endorse gender equality yet, for example, compel your daughter to "dress like a girl" or to revere princesses and you come to realize your error, the appropriate internal response upon this realization is shame. The very important thing about shame is that it is a moral sensibility that allows us to self-regulate; rational persons can appreciate the degree to which their moral personalities, so to speak, are split and, being rational, can move to reconcile themselves accordingly.

The difficult thing about shame is that various features of our character can interfere with an honest reckoning. Sometimes, pride interferes with moral enlightenment; other times, callousness works to scrub away moral sensitivity; while yet other times, simple ignorance precludes our ability to act and believe rightly. When this is the case it is necessary that others intervene in our moral lives by providing a reminder of our failings. Douglass and Wells built careers on this very basic goal—they served constantly and consistently as America's conscience. When Douglass stood before his Rochester assembly and reminded his audience that Independence Day, ideally meant for all subjugated persons in America, was only applicable to the whites who owned black bodies and souls, he was mapping out a shameful state of affairs. When Wells exposed the Curve Lynching, for which the price was exile, she presented to America a mirror of its own hypocrisy. One type of hypocrisy is the belief that men and women can succeed by their own efforts, so long as the success of blacks does not compete with that of whites. Another is that the press is essential to freedom, even as it fails to convey the facts of unwarranted black murders by private citizens and state authorities.

Sound familiar? It is troubling that past the twenty-first century mark, we are required to revisit the themes of hypocritical liberty and unjustifiable black death. But in a country in which brown and black Americans are over-policed and over-surveilled and in which they are far more likely to face police brutality, it is time to return to the past. The idea of shameful publicity is something distinct from post-hoc protest. It is an offensive rather than defensive strategy that mobilizes the ideal of America as we seem to endorse it against the failure of America as it actually is. Its goal is to shed light on institutions whose mandates are carried out unfairly with impunity, to the great detriment of black lives.

This kind of disposition toward our society is rejected by many, even some black American intellectuals. Thomas Sowell, senior fellow at Stanford University's Hoover Institute, is prominent among them. Having spent a career deriding ideas like racial and identity politics, and paying homage to the ideal of America even as that ideal remains a fiction for almost 12 percent of Americans, Sowell has been vehement in his criticism of progressive politics. His tactics are tried and true among conservatives: to identify blacks' desire for fair opportunities as a desire for handouts while celebrating all other Americans' ill-gotten gains being the result of hard work, to hallow the memories of our founders' quest for liberty while stating that black American slavery was not especially historically distinct, and to call this view patriotic. Finally, once the grounds are set, he advocates charging those with complaints against the status quo as seeking to "dismantle America." Apologies, among many decent things, seem to especially disturb Sowell. He writes, "Public apologies to people who are not owed any apology have become one of the many signs of mushy thinking in our times. So are apologies for things that somebody else did. Among the most absurd apologies have been apologies for slavery by politicians."[1] Sowell's resistance to such instances of public repentance is his belief that they threaten to undermine personal responsibility, since the apologies do not track what the politicians have actually done. But this view is deeply confused.

One way the view is confused is that it conveniently erases the relationship between political representation and history. A sitting politician is an agent of the US government, and the history of the US government is steeped in the harms of slavery, some of which remain with us, as evidenced in the resilience of systemic racial inequality that parallel forms of physical abuse and economic disadvantage. So when that politician apologizes, she or he is in fact taking responsibility for her or his civic station as a public servant. The other way the view is confused is that it suppresses the value of symbols, something Sowell seems otherwise invested in when he reveres "American values." The point of an apology isn't always to, in fact, personally take responsibility for something to which you have a causal relationship—rather, it is to express solidarity and sympathy with those who are owed some form of acknowledgment and who, without that acknowledgment, are justified in feeling alienated.

In maybe surprising fashion, shameful publicity is more forceful than apology-seeking, and it elides Sowell's weak objections. Shameful publicity sets the terms of moral and ethical acknowledgment on those acceptable to complainants. Moreover, apologies themselves often work to dissolve ongoing responsibility even when the effects of the problem being acknowledged persist. Offerings of apologies may mollify but they rarely correct states of affairs on their own; moreover, it is often unclear whether the offering of an apology effectively modifies one's moral capacities. This is not the case with shame—shame necessarily demands a reckoning. It is an elegant and intimate form of the very thing Sowell demands in his calls for personal responsibility. Moreover, shameful publicity demands an upstanding correspondence between politics and the polity. As Sowell himself writes elsewhere, "There is nothing automatic about the way of life achieved in this country.... It didn't just happen. People made it happen."[2] Yes, they did, and should be reminded of it at every chance.

COUNTERCOLONIZATION OF THE WHITE IMAGINATION

Commentators on racial inequality often speak about bias or prejudice as attitudinal end states that result in harmful behaviors, which is, of course, a legitimate charge. However, the conversation that is had much less often in public circles is the one seeking to better understand the image whites have of black Americans. How do white Americans imagine the kind of lives blacks aspire toward and the habits they employ in their everyday dealings? What is their image of the bonds of love that clearly affect black relationships of all sorts? Importantly, do white Americans have a decent sense of how blacks see American society?

This is an important conversation to be had, but consistent with a radical ethics, blacks needn't and probably shouldn't wait for that conversation to take place; the course of American history cautions against further patience and urges, rather, a proactive stance. The cues for such a stance were provided in the course of the Harlem Renaissance.

As I put it in chapter 2, a main aim of the Renaissance was to, in effect, (re)present the image and character of blacks apart from the biases that were applied to slaves. In particular, Hughes and Hurston culled the expression and patronage of everyday city blacks and country blacks to work up stories, theater, and poetry that argued for the depth, complexity, and sophistication of black American culture and heritage. If one of the major issues was that blacks were not seen as possessing a legitimate history or deep culture, then that sensibility would have to be instilled in white minds through a vigorous and rigorous pursuit of arts and letters. Though blacks have been and remain marginalized from many high-paying professions and the academy, it has always been the case that whites are willing and often eager to consume black arts. The lesson from Hughes and Hurston is that a key to fighting racism is to try and reach a fundamental cause of it: the image of blacks whites hold in their mind. And because that image of blacks often serves to legitimate or, at least, to provide a sense of comfort to whites' privileged status in America, it seems a good idea to colonize their imaginations—to take up a place in their capacity to envision and revise the world in order to compel them toward a conception of black life they would not form on their own.

To get clearer as to why this particular lesson is so urgent, consider Randall Kennedy's recent endorsement of black respectability politics. As a renowned and respected professor at Harvard Law School, Kennedy has spent a lifetime navigating the halls of privilege that have historically sidelined, and continue today to sideline, wider minority representation. I offer this not as a side-note biographical observation but as something that matters to our reasoning on the uses and misuses of respectability—Kennedy clearly has achieved something in his life by deploying a particular strategy, and is in a position to counsel younger blacks on uplift. But this makes his recommendations even more problematic.

The central aim of respectability politics is very basic and entirely understandable—to present to whites a persona that is beyond judgment and reproach in order to successfully navigate and avoid the various pitfalls and disadvantages blacks otherwise face in a society littered with white privilege. Respectability politics is, in the first instance, a survival strategy. In Kennedy's own words, "[A]ny marginalized group should be attentive to how it is perceived. The politics of respectability is a tactic of public relations that is, per se, neither necessarily good nor necessarily bad."[3] Kennedy's language here is crucial—"any marginalized group should be attentive to how it is perceived." When we state the problem in that way, we observe the first problem with respectability politics—it leaves the flow of power undisturbed. On the view of respectability politics, my actual character—whether I am a thief or a charitable person, whether I am a conniver or upstanding—is irrelevant. If at the moment of my presentation to any white person I don the appearance of the kind of black person whites *associate* with deviance, then it becomes my responsibility to meet their vision of a "proper" black person in order to escape their probing judgment, or their violence.

It's entirely uncontroversial to note the deep unfairness and inequality in this dynamic for nothing in it allows a black American to set the terms of the engagement. Moreover, it now pressures blacks to view themselves through whites' eyes, thereby voluntarily reproducing the problem of twoness Du Bois so eloquently explicated in *The Souls of Black Folks*. This poses an additional psychological and often affective burden to perceive oneself as a person of worth and dignity. What are my resources and reasons for fully valuing myself if I have to set aside my preferences in order to move through society unmolested? The complementary critical point in this dynamic is that while blacks are left doing all the work of artificially short-circuiting whites' biases, white Americans' moral cognition remains entirely untouched— they are required to do no work in revising the very improper modes of perception and valuation they engage in every time they begin to work up an assessment of a black person they see or meet.

This very brief set of reflections exposes Kennedy's conclusion as deeply problematic. For the tactical deployment of a politics of respectability to be, per se, neither good nor bad, it would have to be the case that blacks do not pay a price for baseline respect as citizens in the course of practicing such a politics. But that is not what happens. Rather, the starting point for any black American practicing the politics of respectability lies outside the boundaries of self-determination and begins in the territory of white perception.

This is a state of affairs to which a great many of the Harlem Renaissance artists would have objected. Once one accepts what is required by the politics of respectability one cedes a crucial ground of contestation—the content of imagination that feeds into ethical conviction that in turn informs how we act in the world. When Hurston writes of her irritation that whites consistently expect her self-narrative to be sorrowful, she is bristling at the attempt to truncate the range of her human interests and emotions. Her white interlocutors fail to recognize that maybe she has interests not related to racial struggle; it does not occur to her white interlocutor that perhaps Hurston is more interested in being invested in moments of joy rather than melancholy. When Hurston creates in Janie Crawford a woman who outlives two husbands and who is economically and spiritually liberated, she is setting the stage for her own pronouncement that she cannot begin to fathom how anyone does not appreciate the pleasure of her company. Hurston, in this instance, is using her art to lay the groundwork for a refiguring of how she desires to be perceived by white Americans and how she hopes black women generally can break free from either the expectation of black sexual predation or the stereotype of the "mammie"—a woman whose job is to care for the well-being of whites, especially their children. Indeed, Janie is a character who is defined neither by her reproductive organs nor by a capacity for motherly nurturing, but by the robustness of her nondependent spirit.

It turns out, then, that the desire of Renaissance artists comes into close conflict with the politics of respectability and, indeed, recommends something more radical—an uncompromised effort to put forth one's own preferred self-presentation. You will have noticed by now that the previous paragraphs have been heavily populated with visual language, like "presentation." This is consonant with Hughes's claim in "I, Too" that the day he makes his way to the table with the whites who exclude him, they will see that he is beautiful. My usage of visual language is no coincidence in my disagreement with Kennedy. Kennedy affirms, "We know intuitively that our appearance affects the treatment we receive. Image does not wholly dictate response, but often it makes a difference." His supporting examples are wholly sensible ones. For example, when TV personalities appear for their shows, they are often well-dressed in suits. But such examples are misleading. People who dress to impress in such situations are playing by the rules of a much more general and less offensive game—that of situational awareness of one's audience and coparticipants. However, when blacks are counseled to constantly be mindful of their presentation, they are being asked to move beyond situational awareness to mollification and self-abandonment. It is one thing to dress for a job interview; it is quite another to dress—to present oneself—to simply be part of American society. The burden of judgment imposed by the politics of respectability can easily colonize black minds. The women and men of the Harlem Renaissance would, among other strategies, urge us to countercolonize the white imagination, where a struggle for presentational liberation is one promising site in a struggle for social equality.

UNCONDITIONAL
SELF-POSSESSION

"Only the BLACK WOMAN can say, 'when and where I enter, in the quiet, undisputed dignity of my womanhood, without violence and without suing or special patronage, then and there the whole *Negro race enters with me*."[4] This quote is very much worth revisiting. Its boldness is difficult to overvalue. Consider the feat of self-possession Cooper accomplishes in these thirty-seven words. First, there is the capitalization of "black woman"—a visual cue to readers that those two words are meant to be emphasized together. That cue is preceded by a definitive declaration: only; no one else can accomplish what will happen later in the statement—only the BLACK WOMAN. The remainder of the statement is unsettling in its quiet demandingness. Predating the contemporary usage of "safe spaces" by more than a century, Cooper juxtaposed the sanctity of a woman's respect against the violence it often faces, or the fact that women often have to petition for safety and noninterference. When a black woman can move about society as such, she brings with her a monumental bundle—the whole of the black race.

Now contrast Cooper's declaration with that made by Brown University economist Glenn Loury, in 2015, on the matter of "black lives matter" versus "all lives matter": "Incanting 'Black Lives Matter' rather than 'All Lives Matter' hardly constitutes advocating 'racial justice,' in my view. Indeed, I see the making of such verbal concessions as a kind of cheap grace. These genuflections ask very little of the (white) politicians or their (white) voters."[5] This collection of educated words misses a crucial point of the current movement generally and stands in need of a lesson on unconditional self-possession. Rather than demand a bended knee, present-day activists and intellectuals supporting the #BlackLivesMatter movement have extended the call for Americans to acknowledge the very basic idea that blacks are worthy of a respect that whites take for granted. Thus, when activists incant "black lives matter," they are in fact asking a great deal of white politicians and white voters. Specifically, they are campaigning for whites to see blacks for the persons they are and as deserving the inviolable rights embodied in personhood. To call such a demand a "cheap grace" is to express compassion as resentment and call it uplift. Yet, there is nothing instructive in Loury's recommendation, save a strategy to cede the grounds of the democratic demand for respect and acknowledgment.

It's possible that the clumsiness of Loury's statement has to do with a more pointed principle that must be elucidated within the #BlackLivesMatter movement, as well as outwardly to wider America—a more radical principle embodied in Cooper's statement.

The movement and its supporters—black and white—have done, I think, what can be done to respond clearly to the criticism that activists should celebrate that all lives matter. The use of "black" as a predicate of the moral mandate the slogan represents is not meant to suggest that black lives matter more than others. Rather, it claims that in point of fact, across American history, black lives have not mattered very much but are nevertheless morally owed equal standing, so the polity must be reminded of the basic fact that instead of not mattering, black lives do matter. It can be baffling to reasonable people that such an essential point can be made. One strategy would be to follow Loury's unfortunate recommendation that blacks retreat from the strong claim that black lives matter. That would be a momentous error. But I also think it is an error to merely hold the essential ground activists have claimed. It might be time to follow Cooper's lead and get even bolder by suggesting to America: only the BLACK AMERICAN can say, "when and where I enter, in the quiet, undisputed dignity of my personhood, without violence and without suing or special patronage, then and there the whole *of American democracy enters with me.*"

In formulating this stronger claim, we not only follow Cooper's lead but build on the principle of shameful publicity and the countercolonization of the white imagination (which blacks can and sometimes tragically do adopt as their own) with Lorde's help. What has gone wrong in the claim that "all lives matter" is not that it is false. Rather, it is beside the point as a matter of both hubris and lack of imagination. Further, it obfuscates the question of identity altogether as well as the different kinds of value placed on various identities. Indeed, Lorde's insistence to hold her identity markers close to her was a way of showing that indeed many kinds of lives matter. But she also saw that black life, on account of it being black, faced particularly trying challenges. That continues today. On the one hand, some cannot comprehend how blacks could be so bold as to claim that their lives ought to be respected; on the other, some cannot imagine that America is the kind of nation that perpetrates the evils that blacks experience and describe. The amendment to Cooper's statement signals something fundamental. American democracy cannot claim for itself the title of a liberal, well-ordered democracy so long as blacks are so often killed with impunity by private citizens and state agents, or as long as they earn lower incomes simply because of their skin color, or as long as their children receive substandard education because of their ancestors. Indeed, the ideal of democracy, even if imperfectly practiced, requires that one's life chances not hinge on entirely arbitrary and irrational features like race.

Nor can they hinge on features like gender and sexual orientation. There is a big risk in amending Cooper's statement in the way I have, for it seems to once again sideline the very necessary attention she intended to draw to the importance of gender inequality. No such thing is meant to be the result. Quite to the contrary, having engaged her work as we have in chapter 3, I have taken as settled her point that racial equality cannot be genuine if black women are not central and equal partners in articulating what needs to count as racial justice. The same holds true with respect to sexual orientation. One's sense of uncompromising self-possession hinges on nothing else than one's own affirmation of the markers of identity that give specific shape to the inequality and oppression one suffers. My use of "black American" as an amendment to Cooper's bold statement takes for granted that a multiplicity of identities can and must be accommodated within the general struggle for racial justice. In Lorde's own poignant words, "The increasing attacks upon lesbians and gay men are only an introduction to the increasing attacks upon all Black people, for whatever oppression manifests itself in this country, Black people are potential victims."[6] That Lorde understands the special vulnerability of black Americans, while Loury does not, even as he and others see blacks left lying in the streets by the police, is all the more reason for black Americans to take absolute possession of their humanity in the course of asking others to recognize the worth of their humanity.

UNFRAGMENTED COMPASSION

Some commentators on the state of black America since the "success" of the Civil Rights Act of 1964 have been cold and unthinking in their criticisms of blacks. They have taken up standard white conservative criticisms of black fatherless homes or inner-city cultures of failure and violence, which are themselves redeployments of liberal ideology in the strictest sense of that term. All of these arguments imagine 1964 as a sharp historical break that rightly introduced a no-more-excuses rhetoric—blacks were given equality, and look how they are wasting it! However, other commentators have been clever in channeling this line of argument. John McWhorter, for example, argues in his prominent book *Winning the Race: Beyond the Crisis in Black America* that blacks have a debilitating mindset he terms "therapeutic alienation." Whereas some black conservatives deny the role of racism today, McWhorter is amenable (though not eager) to conceding that blacks can suffer from discrimination as a sociopolitical blight on our society. However, he thinks something has gone terribly wrong among the American black population's deployment of race: "Most blacks were more interested in fighting the concrete barrier of legalized *discrimination* than the abstract psychological happenstance of *racism*."[7] When blacks, on his view, began to focus on racism (though I'm not sure when it is McWhorter thinks blacks *did not* act against racism), they moved from the realm of complaints actionable through policy to the realm of ideas that demand no action. This is because, as he put it a few lines later, the offense of racism is "hazy." But more than muddle the boundaries of our complaints, the move to race seemed to overwhelm the problem, prompting the therapeutic response of black alienation.

The clever part of McWhorter's argument is that he thinks blacks' therapeutic choice was foisted on them by white liberals, thereby making blacks triply victimized by discrimination, whites, and themselves.

Apart from McWhorter's condescending tone, there is a great deal to intellectually disavow in his analysis. For one thing, for a very significant stretch of history—certainly predating the civil rights movement McWhorter means to reference—blacks have discussed their plight in terms of racism and certain actionable complaints, such as discrimination. Indeed, it is the charge of racism that gives a particular moral weight to the formal crime of discrimination. Most unfortunate in McWhorter's claim is that blacks are too psychologically fragile to renounce racism and too psychologically needy to relinquish the white liberal gift of the idea of "alienation." I want to turn to our thinkers in focusing on this aspect of McWhorter's argument, since his historical claim cannot withstand any scrutiny whatsoever.

The love ethic propounded by Baldwin and King, despite differences in certain emphases in their respective articulation of it, depends on two very crucial principles: self-respect and other-regarding sympathy. One fights for justice out of self-respect, and one withholds resentment and violence out of sympathy. The more radical principle I want to draw from both thinkers is that of unfragmented compassion. What do I mean?

A clear implication of what Baldwin and King thought about love is that it requires sacrifice, vulnerability, acceptance of risk, and courage. When we attempt to love, we are prepared to make our interests secondary when necessary, express our deepest desires, accept the possibility of rejection, and accept on an unconditional basis the reasonable responsibilities close partnership demands of us. But all of this presumes something that neither Baldwin nor King made explicit. Indeed, what is required by the love ethic is the idea of the whole person or of personal wholeness. What I mean by this is simple but urgent.

The sacrifices we make for love sometimes require that what we prefer to be true about the world needs to be compromised with a view to accommodating others' preferences, needs, desires, or wishes. Our vulnerability in these moments is that of a person who *could* be injured by others' words and deeds no matter how good we have been to others; the integrity and care with which we act toward others is never a guarantee of being treated in kind, but that is also never a good enough reason to not try to act with integrity and care, to act from love. Rational people know this and accept the possibility of disappointment. Doing so often requires overcoming the picture we often have of ourselves as already fully prepared to meet the complex demands of ethical life. In overcoming this self-image, we open the possibility of cultivating more resilient and flexible attitudes and beliefs about what we owe others as well as ourselves. None of this can be accomplished successfully if we lack integrity—if we lack personal wholeness. To have personal wholeness means to know our own strengths and weakness as well as our own tolerance for others' vices, and finally, the developed temerity to consistently assess our relationships with intelligence.

The idea of personal wholeness is deeply significant as it allows the more radical ethical stance of unfragmented compassion. The reason McWhorter's argument is not only wrong but condescending is that it denies blacks' ability to identify the patronizing language and ideas that white liberals use to manipulate black interests. It also denies blacks' own ability to hold genuine resentment for black inequality, whether it results from overt or implicit racism.

Unfragmented compassion is an ideal that ethically extends the idea of personal wholeness. As a virtue, compassion recommends that we take up affective and rational positions to comprehend—not adopt or internalize—other's difficulties. The kind of love propounded by Baldwin and King urged us to view whites' simultaneous denial of their own, and black, humanity with compassion; their coarseness and callowness in doing so was a betrayal of their capacities to do what is required by standard ideas of goodness and rightness. Similarly, we can be compassionate toward ourselves. A central component to the love ethic of these two thinkers is that one must resist demeaning images foisted upon us by the legacy of white supremacy and persistent stereotypes, that one must resist the despair real everyday inequality can impose on our existence, that one must resist raw rage no matter how justified. To give oneself over to rage is to decisively cede the grounds of mutual understanding that is necessary for any functioning society.

My idea of unfragmented compassion is meant to do something very particular. It draws a bridge across the chasm between black self-regard and compassion for white Americans. If the claim "black lives matter" is meant to raise black lives to an equal status with white lives, it is necessarily true that we must keep white humanity in view and, in doing so, observe, listen, and be prepared to enter into relationships defined by reciprocity and mutual regard. However, that claim also asks that each black American understand that, no matter the racially lopsided state of American society, there is no rational reason to forgo one's own interests in a good life. What is urgent in the idea of unfragmented compassion is that compassion introduces human kindness when, for example, we come to learn that another's bad beliefs are a matter of childhood inculcation rather than an intentionally formed desire to articulate those bad beliefs. It also justifies moments of extreme coolness when our compassion for others opens us to the risk of disrespect or worse. Here, the ability to close oneself off from others in moments that justify that closing illustrates to white Americans that our sense of self-worth is nonnegotiable. The value of being able to move between these stances and dispositions cannot be overstated. On the one hand, it sets a standard of both sympathy and potential militancy toward others, thus defining the acceptable boundaries of ethical and political engagement under conditions of inequality. On the other, it reclaims from others the chance to say that blacks only use racism as a form of therapy and wounded attachment. Rather it allows blacks to say, without qualification, that their interest is the justice that has been withheld from them for over three centuries, and that no amount of semantic jabbing can puncture the veil of enlightenment that underwrites that interest, even if others have chosen to remove theirs.

WHAT OF THE FUTURE?

When I was young and enjoyed science fiction (I still enjoy it), I remember there being two competing visions of the future. One vision had me believe that the future would necessarily be better. Technology would make our lives easier and humanity would be sufficiently enlightened to put a stop to practices and habits that cause us and others suffering. The other vision was a stark contrast. In this vision, society was on the verge of collapsing, if it hadn't already. In this scenario, we had become overly reliant on technology and forfeited our own capacities for judgment and labor. Crucially, we had become morally lazy and cruel in our competition for supremacy among ourselves, and, failing to see the coming calamity begotten by human hubris, we created the conditions for apocalypse.

During those young and innocent years, I saw the twenty-first century as a marker of the future populated by so much science fiction. It certainly seemed to me to be far enough away to be "the future." So, here we are, one-and-a-half decades into the future, and what do we have to say for ourselves? Surely, so far as it concerns certain marvels, such as the remarkable miniaturization of electronics and the proliferation of persistent communications networks, this is the future of which at least some of us dreamed. Being able to video-call a family member while on a speeding train was the stuff of my boyhood fantasies, and now I can do it.

But what of social issues? The answer here is both saddening and hopeful. In *The New Jim Crow*, Michelle Alexander powerfully and persuasively argued that institutions like our carceral system are reproducing racial terror in just the ways Jim Crow–era social practices did.[8] Indeed, as I look upon what feels like the unending trend of police violence against blacks, the stubborn forms of material inequality that themselves stunt the life chances of black adults and children, it can sometimes seem that now—in the twenty-first century, the future to my innocent past—is shaping up to resemble some of the worst of the visions of what ignorance and hubris bring to human society. The inability to embrace each other as having sacred lives worth every effort to honor and protect enables the vices of selfishness and hatred. These were the preconditions for apocalypse, and when I observe the number of black deaths captured on our modern marvels of technology, I feel a deep foreboding for the status of black humanity in America.

But is there reason for hope? On that winter day in 2012 when Trayvon Martin was unjustifiably killed by George Zimmerman, a chain of events was set off that defines our present. Martin was by far not the first unarmed black person to be killed with impunity in America. But in the course of events, three women decided that not one more black person's life would be taken without America being forced to answer the question that black intellectuals have been asking for more than one-and-a-half centuries: do black lives in America matter or not? From Douglass to King, the demands have been made for whites to relinquish their privilege and genuinely see, hear, and embrace black humanity. That demand has been made with the tools of shame, imagination, self-care, and love. Today, we must heed our forebears and press more radically and urgently the case they set before the American people, whether they will choose to strive for the ideal of a fair and humane democracy or whether they will accept the failure of sympathy and regard we so regularly witness in our media. Do or do not black lives matter? We still wait for America's response. But the question has been asked, the conversation is being demanded, and there are yet other futures to be written if we so will it.

BLACK, BLUES, AND AMERICA

Amiri Baraka and Angela Davis on the Freedom to Be Black

[I]t was assumed that anybody could sing the blues. If someone had lived in this world into manhood, it was taken for granted that he had been given the content of his verses.

—AMIRI BARAKA, *Blues People*

The first condition of freedom is the open act of resistance.

—ANGELA DAVIS, *Lectures on Liberation*

ON JUNE 9, 2020, GEORGE FLOYD was sent home. More than five hundred people attended his funeral at The Fountain of Praise church in Houston, Texas, which itself followed a memorial attended by more than six thousand people. There was mourning and there was joyous music, despair and hope. There was remembrance of a life and there was prophecy of a nation buckling under the weight of racial hypocrisy. June 9 was spent as many days honoring a black death in America have been spent over the centuries—full of sadness and also resilience. Another black life had been lost to the hands of hatred, yet the living in attendance would go on resisting the denial of black humanity. Another black soul was sent home on a sea of anger and love that has persistently colored black folks' experience of America for more than nearly four centuries.

The story of Floyd's death, thus of the remembrance of his life, is eerily and tragically familiar to us by now. In the early evening of May 25, 2020, Floyd entered a local convenience store—Cup Foods—to buy cigarettes. He was a regular at the store and had no previous history of causing trouble on his visits. On this night, the employee who sold Floyd a pack of cigarettes went to his supervisor claiming that Floyd had paid with a counterfeit twenty-dollar bill. Oddly, in more than a year since Floyd's death, this fateful incident has receded from the story of Floyd's death,[1] and neither has it ever been established whether Floyd indeed tried to pass counterfeit currency.

I emphasize this because it draws our attention to the very thin thread attaching black life to society and the slight amount of punitive force needed to sever the connection. Police arrived less than ten minutes after the store supervisor called to report the alleged fake currency. At that point Floyd was sitting in a car outside the store with friends. Though he seemed to pose no threat and his supposed offense was a nonviolent crime, the police ordered him out of the vehicle at gunpoint; he complied. He went stiff, however, as officers attempted to put him in the police vehicle with his hands cuffed behind his back. Floyd told them that he was claustrophobic. Soon more officers arrived on the scene. Now Floyd was lying face down on the ground, hands still cuffed behind his back. It was at this moment that Officer Derek Chauvin got on the ground and placed his knee on Floyd's neck. Over the next nine minutes Floyd exclaimed and pleaded that he couldn't breathe, called for his mother and asked that she tell his kids that he loved them, and, finally, said to Chauvin,

"You're going to kill me, man." Then Floyd did indeed die under the knee of that man as onlookers video-recorded the murder. Chauvin can be seen in the video looking around at the crowd, who was asking him to please get his knee off Floyd's neck. Chauvin looked almost surprised that anyone could be complaining about the way he was casually but surely snatching away Floyd's life.

In recounting the circumstances of Floyd's death, it is easy to develop the Nietzschean sense of "eternal recurrence of the same."[2] After all, wasn't it just a handful of years earlier that another police officer choked Eric Garner in plain view on a city street for trying to sell cigarettes? Floyd's story is abysmally normal in American society, and it is this normalcy that invites us to explore Angela Davis's and Amiri Baraka's lives and writings in this chapter. It is this normalcy that compels us to appreciate the centrality of blues scholarship in both their corpuses, which I will show has a close relationship to a question every black and brown American inevitably faces: What does it mean to *be* black or brown in America? This is not a question about how one achieves the American dream or gets a job, though these kinds of consideration bear on the question. But rather, what is it to live in brown skin in a country that regularly expresses violence toward people like me simply because my life is in brown skin rather than white skin?

In *Blues People: Negro Music in White America*, Amiri Baraka writes, "[O]ne of the most persistent traits of the Western white man has always been his . . . assumption that his system and ideas about the world are the most desirable, and further, that people who do not aspire to them, or at least think them admirable, are savages or enemies."[3] There is a twofold significance to this statement. First, consider what the statement itself argues—that a form of white supremacy is ideational. There is, on Baraka's view, a white framing for understanding the world that is hostile to other ways of understanding the world. When some other way of understanding the world surfaces among another group—black people, in this case—they are to be seen not as worthy people from whom something might be learned but rather, precisely because their ideas are different and *their* own, must be considered lesser and possibly dangerous. This means that for reasons that have nothing to do with the ideas themselves but because the ideas are situated differently, in other, darker bodies, those bodies are the immediate target of suspicion. The very idea of being considered an enemy opens the door to experiencing violence.

The second significance is broader in scale and, in some ways, more fundamental. Baraka indicts "Western" whites. That adjective—Western—is important because it signifies a cultural and historical milieu celebrated because of the widely held belief, among us Westerners, that what makes the West exceptional are our enlightened notions of learning and toleration. The very idea of "the West" itself depends on the triumph of the open and critically inquiring mind over the closed and ignorant one. Yet, following Baraka, the Western white man, wherever blacks are concerned, has chosen ignorance, which itself has begotten belligerence. The second notable characteristic, then, is that this argument is centered in Baraka's book about blues music, a genre of music of which Angela Davis notes, "[T]he vast disappointment that followed emancipation . . . created a discourse that represented freedom in more and immediate and accessible terms [for blacks]."[4] Thus, the blues and, later, jazz music stand as a kind of cultural counterstatement to the white tendency to truncate and eviscerate black presence. One way to appreciate the blues is that it points to the tragedy of America—a place meant for a better and higher purpose but that fails on account of something insubstantial and, literally, unreal: race. This is the opposite of enlightenment triumphalism and naturally has had dire consequences for the integrity of our democratic experiment, as George Floyd fatally learned.

What follows in this chapter is an exploration of ideas during the Black Power era—a historically brief but conceptually and culturally explosive moment when the fight for civil rights was elevated to a fight for the right to proud blackness. It was a moment when formal (yet still uneven) access to voting was deemed insufficient. The Black Panther Party for Self-Defense in Oakland, California, was, for example, agitating in theory for the fall of capitalism. And in practice its members, while legally armed, were standing up to local police forces used to visiting terror on urban neighborhoods. The terrain of Black Power politics itself has been explored in other important work.[5] My aim here is to channel the heat of the Black Power era through the early productive years of Amiri Baraka and Angela Davis. Specifically, I want to explore their own reflections on the possibilities for contemporary radical action by appreciating blues and jazz as precursors to what we would consider, in contradistinction, rightly or wrongly, more formal black thought. The result of this exploration will allow us, in turn, to see Black Lives Matter as a continuation of a blues ethic that maybe has faded from view for all of us and which we might do well to recapture.

BLACK PEOPLE/BLUES PEOPLE

The 1960s was a battleground decade. It began as a last push for the moral soul of America. The 1950s and 1960s nonviolent actions in support of the civil rights movement, most prominently associated with but certainly not solely conceived or led by Martin Luther King Jr., had undeniably produced results. The pressure of King's tactics and his immense following contributed to landmark legislation such as the Civil Rights Act of 1964 and the Voting Rights Act of 1965. Yet there were signs that this legislation was too late for a younger generation of black Americans as well as being suspiciously status quo and abstract; more militant activists wondered about the point of legal rights in a nation whose people did not and might not ever see those legal rights as properly belonging to black Americans, no matter what Congress or the courts said. Alongside these victories, the 1960s was also marked by black uprisings in major cities across the United States. Housing segregation and persistent black poverty accompanied by police harassment and overbearing surveillance of black neighborhoods rendered the lofty congressional legislative victories too distant from the daily struggle to exist while black. It is little wonder, then, that Black Power was moving to the center of blacks' and the rest of the nation's attention.

Indeed, Kwame Ture and Charles Hamilton expressed the increasingly dominant sentiment in their enduring manifesto *Black Power*: "We blacks must respond [to oppression] in our own way, on our own terms, in a manner which fits our temperaments. The definitions of ourselves, the roles we pursue, the goals we seek are our responsibility."[6] This is an orientation to the struggle for genuine freedom that sidesteps the debate over fair laws and instead issues a call for something more basic, more foundational: What is the role of *blackness* in setting the terms of black freedom? But that question, simple as it may seem, required answering another question as well: What *is* blackness? One thing that seemed certain was that whatever the answer to that question, it implied the radical notion that stabilizing and empowering black existence was now prior to shoring up the American democratic project.

As we have seen in earlier chapters, the desire to empower black existence itself was not new. That move for empowerment showed itself in the words and work of Frederick Douglass, the first thinker on our journey in this book. But what *did* change more noticeably in the Black Power era was an increasing distinction between American democracy and *black* freedom. In prior times it was generally taken for granted that black freedom would be a function of increasing assimilation into American institutions and increasing integration into American social life. The Black Power moment was defined in large part by a rejection of the premise that the good of black life depended on the good of American life. But no credo can succeed on rejection alone, and here were visionaries to fill in the positive content of centering black life.

Prominent among these visionaries was Amiri Baraka (earlier, Leroi Jones). Born October 7, 1934, in Newark, New Jersey, Baraka, a poet, dramatist, and essayist, became a leading activist, speaker, and organizer from within the arts to support the more radical black-affirming, antiracist agenda characteristic of the Black Power movement. Yet it would be a mistake to describe Baraka's contributions or ambitions as simply supporting Black Power. It is more appropriate to describe Baraka as lending to Black Power a conceptual infrastructure for imagining emancipation rooted in history and black music, especially blues and jazz. It is this aspect of Baraka's intellectual and political life I will focus on.

The Newark neighborhood of Baraka's childhood, centered on Dey Street, was racially mixed. Given that this was an era of virulent Jim Crow segregationist practices, integration in a northern town might suggest a reason for progressive hopefulness. This was not a fact, however, that would provide any form of existential peace for the young Baraka. In fact, it inevitably led to that Du Bois-ian moment of being forcefully reminded that before anything else, he was black while his friends were white.[7] And like Du Bois, his moment of twoness was delivered by the hands of an innocently cruel white child, when the young Baraka asked his friend Augie to borrow his comb so that he could brush his hair, to which Augie responded, "Don't mix the breeds."[8] For Baraka, "it confirmed some upside-down shit I had in my head. That we were white and black."[9] As a result, "in school [Baraka] developed an interior life that was split obviously like the exterior life."[10] Thus he came early to be confronted with the question of what it was to be black in a white world and what it would take to make a world that would be a suitable home for blackness.

These sorts of moments may jolt a person into a premature sociopolitical maturity, but this was not entirely the case for Baraka. He was distinctly race conscious, but on his own account, his adolescent and early adult years spent as a poet and writer did not reflect much in the way of political involvement or leadership, radical or otherwise. Indeed, it seemed, as can often be the case, Baraka wanted to pursue a vision of art rooted in European sensibilities *as a black man*. And he achieved a small degree of success. All the same, the question of what it meant to *be* black in America would compel him to consider his path more carefully.

The question, for Baraka, was nurtured by music, answered through music, and continuously reformulated because of music. This is the nature of the blues and jazz—to provide within a framework of rules a continual means of creation, exploration, and re-exploration of a motif through both spontaneous individual improvisation as well as collective cooperation to support creation and exploration. In other words, blues and jazz came to represent for Baraka models of emancipation and empowerment, and he took it that more black Americans should come to understand that about the music.

The Music, as Baraka affectionately referred to the bodies of expressivist results known as blues and jazz, seemed to have taken up residence in his mind and soul in his teen years. (Unfortunately, Baraka is not especially keen on keeping temporal tabs in his autobiography through the steady use of calendar year milestones as narrative signposts.) As he became hipper to street life as well as American life, the two-ness introduced by his childhood friend Augie began to more intently poke and prod at Baraka's consciousness. He speaks of making the social rounds at various venues but adds, "[S]ome other kinds of yearnings turned me around. I wanted to go to some other kinds of places, and usually by myself. . . . 'The Music' had got into me and was growing in me and making me hear things and see things. I began to want things. I didn't even know what."[11] Putting it philosophically, The Music was prompting him to explore the boundaries of his agency and the power of his ability to be an author of his life on his own terms. Let's slow down here to grasp how The Music could do this for black Americans.

The first manifestation of The Music we have to understand is the blues, and it will help to have a sense of the cultural contexts out of which the blues emerged. Blues music as it came to be known as a distinct genre of music arose out of slave field songs created while working on southern plantations. But those songs themselves were rooted in expressive and productive practices in African culture. The late musical historian, critic, and educator Robert Palmer notes that into the 1800s, slaves brought to America were largely extracted from Senegal, Gambia, and Guinea. Despite particular regional differences in cultural practices, he also notes an important commonality:

> [M]ost music making [was] group music making, and in group situations the distinction between performers and audience that is so basic in Western music tends to blur or disappear entirely. . . . The structure of the music actively encourages participation, whether it's call and response, in which anyone can join the response, or a method of organization called hocketing[.][12]

I want to emphasize three politically relevant elements in this form of musical expression: its collective nature, its spontaneously creative nature, and its open nature.

To our contemporary sensibilities, the idea of collectively made music is consigned to parochial notions of the musical group or band. We readily perceive that when we see Ben Harper on stage with his band, for example, the resulting product is collective—the music was performed by the band. Yet, while the band on stage is indeed a kind of collective, this is not the same as the publicly collective music to which Palmer is referring. In Palmer's example, and later on the plantation fields, collective music making involved an amorphous group—any persons who happened to be on site when the music was being made—as well as a loosely defined group with only two roles: the person providing the call (and there might be a preferred person to perform this role due to voice loudness or melodiousness) and everyone else providing the response. Which indicates its spontaneous nature. Among the reasons we have so few "work songs" passed down from slave days, prominent is that there were no "songs" as we conceive them today. The "song" of the moment began with the shouter's improvised theme line, which may have been a commentary on the day's weather, the state of the current crops, a recent birth, or something else. And then, collectively, the surrounding participants repeated or responded to the central theme. Finally, participation was egalitarian. Odd as that word may sound when mentioned in the context of a plantation, the idea behind group music making is precisely that anyone who *wanted to participate*, in contrast to those who were qualified to participate, could in fact participate—presence just was qualification. The political corollaries are readily apparent.

A well-ordered democracy, to borrow a phrase from the political philosopher John Rawls,[13] not only depends on appropriate laws and institutions marked by integrity but also must be regulated by a public conception of justice which all affirm and which all know all others affirm. Thus a well-ordered society cultivates civic habits of mutual recognition and a desire to continuously co-author a shared democratic society. Now consider the three features of African music I have pointed out that later inform blues. First, music's collective nature instills in its participants a nonhierarchical observation of each person's legitimate participation in group music making. Second, while democracy is often understood in terms of the steadfastness and persistence of laws, the everyday life of citizens sharing public spaces is anything but static—we must repeatedly negotiate being ourselves among others who have their own sense of purpose and powers of agency. Third, a public democratic life is intended to be open to all proper members of that society; in fact, the prevention of collapse into despotism depends on the open society. In this way, then, we can see that embedded in the prevalent practice of group music making in African cultural forms that came to inform slave hollers, then country blues, classic blues, and subsequently bebop and post-bop/hard bop jazz, are many of the essential elements of democracy. But what if a society is not well-ordered? On Baraka's (and later Davis's) view, these cultural forms can motivate and cultivate attitudes and practices of freedom and emancipation within black Americans. A process that Baraka and Davis themselves undertook.

This call to assess his level of freedom within a racist society rang especially loud in the wake of Baraka's trip to Fidel Castro's Cuba in July 1959. Castro had come to power as prime minister just months before, in February 1959, after close to a decade of struggle—mostly armed—against Fulgencio Batista's government. Batista staged a coup in 1952, after which he canceled elections in which Castro was meant to be a candidate. While Castro had always been a leftist, he had been pushed farther along that end of the political spectrum after discovering Marxism and its criticism of the propertied elite (in any and all societies founded on capitalist private property and industry) and the way they gained sustenance at the expense of the working class through purported exploitation. Crucial to Marxist thinking is the supposition that class revolution comes inevitably once the working class develops a critical consciousness of its historical status as an exploited class. On the Marxist's view, capitalism has so completely reshaped the reality of the proletariat that they often fail to notice their own exploitation, in part because they are too busy competing with each other for income and jobs. The goal for a Marxist—presumably having already achieved class-critical consciousness—is to effectively "wake" their fellow members of the proletariat.[14]

Castro had long enjoyed the backing of Cuba's youth, including its students. And whether or not most Cubans had come into appropriate political consciousness, Baraka's being harangued by his young adult hosts in July 1959—with the Marxist Castro's victory fresh—achieved its ends. In Baraka's own words, "These young people assaulted my pronouncements about not being political. . . . For twelve or fourteen hours on the train I was assailed for my bourgeois individualism."[15] Up to this point in his life, Baraka had certainly considered himself race conscious, but his main preoccupation, his main desire for self-definition was as a poet. This was unacceptable to his interlocutors, likely because it seemed to them that Baraka was indeed political and was choosing to abdicate a more revolutionary consciousness, thus avoiding the responsibility to achieve freedom and an emancipated consciousness. The result of Baraka's experience was a transformative revelation: "As much hot hatred as I could summon for the U.S., its white supremacy, its exploitation, its psychological torture of schizophrenic slaves like myself, I now had to bear the final indignity . . . the indignity and humiliation of defending its ideology, which I was doing in the name of Art. Jesus Christ!"[16] In the immediate aftermath of his return, Baraka's writing projects reflected an intentional pivot toward making and analyzing art through the lens of existential struggle under the conditions of sociopolitical oppression, with The Music as his guide. His first significant attempt was his Obie Award–winning play, *Dutchman,* followed closely by a historically critical reading of the blues in his classic and enduring *Blues People.*

Despite the fact that works of art, especially drama, are usually open to a variety of interpretations, Baraka wrote *Dutchman,* a two-person play, as if wielding a massive blunt instrument. But that is not to say the play lacks intelligence or insight. Let us do the unusual and begin at the end: Lula, a white woman, murders her conversation partner, Clay, a black man, in the final scene. The question is, what could have led to such a breakdown in communication that Clay's murder was the result?

Baraka stages the play on a New York City train, a circulator of people through the arteries of a cosmopolitan city. Clay is already seated when we meet him, and Lula is introduced somewhat lasciviously as she is the object of Clay's observation through the train window at a station stop. Upon boarding, Lula takes a seat beside Clay, and we are warned of her role as provocateur and temptress as she eats apple after apple, offering them to Clay, which, tellingly, he refuses. As they strike up a conversation, Lula insinuates herself into Clay's evening by revealing details of his identity and plans for the night that she shouldn't know. She names his neighborhood, his friends, and predicts the vibe of the party to which he is headed. Clay is by turns alarmed and intrigued and wants to know how she could know these things. Her answer: "I told you I didn't know anything about *you* . . . you're a well known type."[17] Here, Lula reduces Clay's personhood to (racial) tropes and whites' beliefs about the lives of black people. Their conversation proceeds with Lula being in turn sexually provocative and racially condescending, while Clay tries his hand at obliging Lula's performative privilege at saying whatever she desires at his expense, going so far as to welcome the idea of her attending the party with him.

Baraka has set the tension with indelicate melodrama, and it is clear from the outset that this exchange cannot end well. But this seems part of the point: Clay and Lula's time together, metaphorically as The Black American and The White American, cannot end well, because if Clay is "a type," so is Lula—a casually brutal white American whose sense of herself preempts her sense of Clay. After Lula takes one too many liberties and begins to make a spectacle of herself on the train, Clay breaks the illusion of being able to enter into any sort of social transaction with her by launching into an angry and indignant monologue. One of the most important lines he recites is his description of white Americans as "a people of neurotics, struggling to keep from being sane."[18] A neurosis is a mild, non physiologically caused mental illness. What is the neurosis Baraka wants to bring to our attention?

Race is a nonreal social category; it has no legitimate basis in science. Rather, it is a historical creation by which social groups have formed heuristics for classifying themselves and others, which is no offense in itself. But consider: what kind of people use a category such as race to justify the theft, bondage, murder, rape, and exploitation of another kind of people? What kind of people use a category like race to render another group as first usable, then disposable? When seen from this perspective, white racism is indeed a kind of madness, a nonrational set of judgments used to motivate immoral actions with no grounding in reality. And how should we describe the establishment of a nation and an entire regime of social, political, and economic institutions based on this kind of madness? Well, we could say the result is a society that is not well-ordered. But another way is to describe it is as reigned over by "a people struggling to keep from being sane." And indeed, the insanity is so deep that by the end of the monologue, Lula matter-of-factly says "I've heard enough" and plunges a knife into Clay as he reaches over her to get his bags to leave. Baraka rings the final alarm when Lula, looking around the car, merely exclaims "All right!" and the remaining white passengers spring into action, following her directions to dispose of Clay's body; this unfolds as if all the white people on the train were in on the ruse from the beginning, fully prepared for the likely outcome that, one way or another, Clay would meet a grim end. The play ends with another young black man boarding the train, taking a few seats behind Lula. This scene will play out again.

Whether or not Baraka intended it, *Dutchman* provides a blues setting according to the criteria I outlined earlier.[19] The subway is a space for lateral relations providing for spontaneous social life that is marked by its open-to-all nature. Yet the play is more tragedy than anything else—two representatives of social groups at odds hurtling toward disaster as we, the audience as chorus, want to warn Clay to desist, to leave the train before he meets his end. Thus, the blues setting fails, maybe because it does not work unless it is populated by blues people. So, Baraka went on to try to see what such a people were, in the hope of creating more of them.

Dutchman opened an era in Baraka's life that would prove deeply significant for him as well as American culture generally. James Smethurst writes, "When thinking about

Amiri Baraka's emergence as a major literary figure and intellectual figure, two milestones stand out."[20] One is his being a key player in New American Poetry. The second is "his development into the only major black participant in the new wave of jazz criticism of the 1950's and early 1960's."[21] These years marked an important shift for jazz music. The swing and bebop years defined by the innovations of Charlie Parker and Dizzy Gillespie, and pushed along to new horizons by Thelonious Sphere Monk, was giving way to hard bop and free jazz. Miles Davis's *All Blues* of 1959 established a sonic agenda for his own career and, importantly, for the field of jazz music generally. John Coltrane's *Giant Steps* the following year challenged not merely bebop's notion of chord progression but the very way a person could play the tenor saxophone. Here, Coltrane's "sheets of sound" approach to playing his horn set a new benchmark for technical brilliance and harmonic innovation that drew from and then exceeded Charlie Parker's bebop improvisation patterns.

It was into this scene that Baraka, a lifelong fan of jazz, stepped upon his return from Cuba with, we will recall, a greater sense of black radical political purpose and consciousness. Though *Dutchman* won an Obie Award despite its portrayal of racist homicide, Baraka had more directly to say about history, about the way black music told the story of not just black Americans' potential for creative genius but the way the music itself was a result, expression, and form of resistance to blacks' experience in America as an oppressed class of people. So, it is of some note when Smethurst claims, "The appearance of *Blues People* in 1963 is a plausible beginning for when and where cultural studies begin in the United States[.]"[22] And though Trane and Miles were laying the groundwork for further experiments in hard bop and free jazz, Baraka knew that whatever revolutionary spirit these artists were channeling started with the blues.

One way to define the blues is by its formal nature: a genre of music often employing a twelve- or sixteen-bar structure; harmonically, its "blue" sound is given by a chord structure where major scales are altered so that the fifth note is flattened and the seventh note is played in its dominant tonality; melodically, the "tune," whether sung or played on an instrument, is characteristically (but certainly not always) two lines of a repeated phrase or motif, followed by a third-line response to the motif (AAB patterns), with this pattern repeated throughout. But the other way to define the blues, not exclusive of the first, is as a sensibility or outlook or attitude. The blues is as much a mode of *being* as it is a genre of music, and this acknowledgment was Baraka's great contribution to cultural studies.

For Baraka, this question of black being begins at the beginning: what was it for an African to *be* a slave in America?

> When black people got to this country, they were Africans, a foreign people. The customs, attitudes, desires, were shaped to a different place, a radically different time. . . . But to be brought to a country, a culture, a society, that was, and is, in terms of purely philosophical correlatives, the complete antithesis of one's own version of man's life on earth—that is the cruelest aspect of this particular enslavement.[23]

And if one is really seeking the ethical source of the blues, it would seem to be located in Baraka's contention that "[t]he diverse labors of the African, which were the source of [slave work songs in the fields], had been funneled quite suddenly into one labor, the cultivation of the white man's land."[24] This observation has deep political implications.

Culturally, African work songs were dynamic artifacts of collective creativity. Where European music had long been marked by certain formal song structures, African work music was the result of a shared project of the moment through which lateral relations of equal participation were essential—the kind of lateral relations we've noted as being a hallmark of the democratic spirit. But what does it mean for that culture to be exploitatively and violently relocated to the fields of white productivity? The expression of the music doesn't change, but its significance must; field songs were still sites of equal collective spontaneous creation that described a moment in the life of the people making the music. Yet *these* moments were characterized by the moral problematic of one people being the literal property of another, so the music thereby acquires a political character—these are the melodic utterances that are prelude to a desire for freedom expressed collectively for the purpose of mutual support and recognition.

A signature feature of slave work songs (a continuance of African work songs), was call and response, a form of "musical conversation."[25] Call and response was orchestrated reliably but informally in the practice of one person providing the leading line and all those around responding to that line. But Baraka points out a crucial development: the end of slavery set blacks free as individuals who (when this was indeed possible without white supremacist terrorism) worked their own private field alone, sometimes surrounded by family. This also meant more single performers traveling the country, with a very significant benefit: "There could come now to these ex-slaves a much fuller idea of what exactly America was."[26] One way to imagine this new class of mobile black performers is as circulators; as they picked up new lessons about the nature of America, they dispersed them through song, explicitly or implicitly, performing what we might consider a civic democratic function of enhancing discourse.

If we accept that characterization, we note something else worth paying attention to, and that is that the very practice of call and response integral to the ethical texture of work field songs transforms and relocates as well, for what does it mean for one lone performer of the blues to now replicate call and response? The answer begins with the reconstitution of the performance. The blues that arose out of field songs became an art form in the first instance of a solitary performer accompanying themselves, commonly with a guitar. The performer in a sense became both caller and responder, with lines sung, followed by improvised riffs on a guitar (or harmonica early on, later also the piano, and in the case of Louis Armstrong, the trumpet). But maybe equally as impactful was the later practice of performers compelling the audience itself to respond. This was captured popularly and simply in Cab Calloway's 1932 hit, "Minnie the Moocher." He followed a lyric verse with improvised vocalizations that the audience was prompted to repeat. What is important here is not so much that the mechanics could be found in fairly vacuous songs like Calloway's, but rather that the mechanics could be found at all with whites participating eagerly—an exceptional moment when white Americans were eager to repeat anything a black person said.

The turn of the twentieth century saw a number of changes that allowed black art to become central to the American consciousness, not least of which was the rise of radio and increasingly widespread ownership of the means to play records. With this, black Americans found an opportunity to reach the souls of white folks. While in retrospect,

art alone clearly did not fix the deep moral problems plagu-
ing America, it certainly tilled the soil of American imagination. The blues, itself a product of slave musical expression,
had given rise to swing, bebop, and hard bop, each of these in
turn gaining respectably wide audiences among blacks and
whites in America.

In January 1965, John Coltrane released his landmark
album, *A Love Supreme*—a thoroughly modernist performance that appeared to informally conclude the hard-bop
era. The album was motivated by Trane's metaphysical explorations with religious belief and gratitude.[27] *A Love Supreme*
represented nearly a century of development of black art
that arose from the fields and had developed into a sophisticated compositional form that was both homage to that era
and forward-thinking philosophy. But there was nothing at
all metaphysical about the assassination of Malcolm X the
very next month. A black leader who had indeed expressed
supreme love for black humanity in enjoining us to protect it "by any means necessary" had been taken from the
world at the moment when his alternative to King's philosophy of peace and persuasion had impacted black youth. The
strategy of seeking to persuade whites was being displaced
quickly by a call for Black Power, a positive doctrine of black
self-affirmation and pride in the face of abject disrespect and,
often, violence.

Most black leaders of the time came into direct confrontation with this state of affairs. Of these, Angela Davis's
resistant stance to oppressive power in the name of human
equality and a society founded on universal respect has made
her an enduring icon. You might say she very much embodied the blues. Indeed, equally if not more than Baraka, Davis
held the blues up as an essential historical development of

174 | BLACK, BLUES, AND AMERICA

black political consciousness. Something to hold dear during hard times as one worked toward the better. Even if those hard times involved being a fugitive from the law through association with black youth who, in fact, believed they had to emancipate themselves and those close to them—by any means necessary.

BLUES PEOPLE/FREE PEOPLE

When Baraka declared in *Blues People* "The great classic blues singers were women," it was, unfortunately, a rare (and brief) moment during this era when black women were singled out for recognition and praise.[28] A reader of his autobiography, for example, would have a hard time learning just how important black women were to the twentieth-century freedom struggle, especially during the time of Black Power.[29] It is no relief to learn that this failing was common during the civil rights movement and, maybe more problematically, during the years of Black Power specifically. These were years that generated in a more youthful and less patient cohort of black freedom fighters a desire to positively represent blackness as an identity founded in strength and a robust history. Yet, at too few points were women seen as integral to a conception of black strength or having a proper place in past history—or in making new history.

In the final pages of this book, I want to present a slice of Angela Davis's work produced during a time of extreme difficulty for her—and somewhat proximate to the period of Baraka's work we have engaged—to make some important points. First, there is a second part to the story of the blues, following Baraka's, in which the preeminence of women is essential for framing black twentieth-century longings for human recognition, and that Davis's scholarship helps us appreciate. Second, Davis's own reading of the blues is an intellectual extension of her earlier philosophical work on existentialism and freedom from oppression. Here, I want to close out our intellectual journey considering the making of the idea "black lives matter" by provocatively suggesting that Davis's work should be read not only as a call to freedom from white oppression. It should also be read from the point of view of black women who see that black people cannot be free until blackness is also free from patriarchy, black or white or any other kind. On this view, black patriarchy surely informs harmful views and treatment of black women, but it also causes a further degradation of black men themselves, which brings us full circle to Anna Julia Cooper's powerful, maybe prophetic proclamation, "Only the BLACK WOMAN can say, 'when and where I enter, in the quiet, undisputed dignity of my womanhood, without violence and without suing or special patronage, then and there the whole *Negro race enters with me.'*" For Angela Davis, the condition that violence be absent from the black woman's life would be difficult to secure.

Though Davis to this day remains a prominent public intellectual whose work on prison abolition has been read widely, she is probably most famous for the wrong sort of thing: for being a fugitive from the law. On August 7, 1970, Jonathan Jackson—brother to George Jackson, who gained notoriety for his radical political philosophical writings while incarcerated at Soledad Prison, represented in the enduring compilation *Soledad Brother*[30]—along with three inmates attempted to stage an armed breakout during a court appearance. The result was mayhem and death, including that of the presiding judge. The gun Jackson used belonged to Davis, and the police sought her on charges related to the murder and insurrection. Davis fled, distrustful of the police, who, by this time, had been actively involved in anti–Black Power activities, including the suspected assassination of prominent leaders. Though apprehended three months later, Davis was eventually cleared of all charges. She was commonly asked why, if she knew she was innocent, did she run? But the more compelling question is: Why did she feel the need to own a deadly weapon in the first place?

Davis was born a child of the American South in Birmingham, Alabama, to two middle-class parents, on January 26, 1944. Violence was an early part of her life. Her parents were the first black family to move into what would become Davis's childhood neighborhood; as she recalls, "[T]he white people believed we were in the vanguard of a mass invasion": "Almost immediately after we moved there [in 1948] the white people got together and decided on a border line between them and us. . . . If we ever crossed over to their side, war would be declared. Guns were hidden in our house and vigilance was constant."[31] The bombings began in 1949, when local racists decided the best defense was a good offense. This represented a campaign to drive out the growing number of black residents. With macabre irony, the residential area came to be referred to as "Dynamite Hill."

Like Baraka, Davis came to a realization in her younger years that something about the ways and means of white racism was affecting the texture of black life in America: "The inner-directed violence which was so much a part of our school lives at Tuggle [Middle School] accelerated at Parker [High School] to the point where it verged on fratricide."[32] Where Baraka had been invited to reconsider his social situation through the clumsiness of a young friend's racism, Davis here is drawing our attention to a larger parallel relationship—the way whites deployed violence toward blacks on account of blackness, and the way blacks turned that violence on themselves on account of rage that could be directed nowhere else except inwardly and between black Americans.

The impact and effects of this misdirected rage are worth considering, especially in relation to the idea of freedom, because the reason for the rage is precisely that those living under oppression are keenly aware not merely that they are not free but that they are kept from being free and are preferred as being unfree. Indeed, Davis opens her "Lectures on Liberation" this way: "One of the most acute paradoxes present in the history of Western society is that while on a philosophical plane freedom has been delineated in the most lofty and sublime fashion, concrete reality has always been permeated with the most brutal forms of unfreedom, of enslavement."[33] The paradox is not hard to fathom— one cannot consistently espouse freedom and unfreedom at the same time, unless, that is, one thinks race alone disqualifies one from freedom. But once we consider that the notion of modern freedom becomes bound up with the framework of natural and human rights, then one is left with only two possible conclusions: either blacks are not to be considered human, or no one is in fact free because the very idea of the West has been constructed on a falsehood to which we are all shackled, and it's just that some of us far worse off than others. More likely, both are true simultaneously. But in the lectures Davis emphasizes the way this possibility impacts black lives.

Davis's approach is informed by a trinity of thinkers wherein Marx is at the pinnacle. He is worth revisiting for just a moment. We have seen that Marx's enduring contribution to contemporary revolutionary ideals is tethered to his critique of Western capitalism and its exploitation of workers. But underneath that criticism is a phenomenological argument, itself indebted to Hegel: world history moves in dialectical cycles, whereby two opposed historical drives compete with each other and resolve into a third, synthetic option. Marx leveraged this view to argue that the modern era would be defined by a struggle between workers and capitalism, and that a workers' revolution would resolve history in favor of a postcapitalist non-property-owning world where we each are free to dispose of our time and efforts as we see fit with no concern for profit motive or wage earning.

This is worth understanding because underneath the romantic veneer of revolution is a powerful philosophical tendency to reframe the world not as merely the incidental collective of individual choices but rather to see those choices as only partially free depending on where one is positioned within particular systems of power. For Marx, the property-owning capitalists are hemmed in by capitalism but are free *within* capitalism, whereas workers are simply not free in any way, until, that is, they can begin to develop a critical consciousness of their historical situation and begin to imagine how to unmake that situation. It is this movement of ideas leading to the preceding conclusion that was attractive to black radicals of the 1960s and 1970s. But Davis, who by the time she delivered her lectures was already committed to Marxism, engaged the ideas of another thinker influenced by Marx: Jean-Paul Sartre.

Sartre was himself a Marxist, but he was concerned about the possibilities of the dialectical process for personal freedom rather than thinking at the sweeping level of social classes on the stage of world history. As an existentialist, Sartre pursued the problematic of how each of us accomplishes or is impeded in the accomplishment of achieving full personhood in the midst of our varied contexts.[34] The idea of the Marxist dialectic gets miniaturized to deal with the more individualized Sartrean question of what it means to be, to exist, and reflecting on what we can do to better our being and existing.

Thus, it is significant when Davis argues that "if the theory of freedom remains isolated from the practice of freedom or rather is contradicted in reality, then this means that something must be wrong with the concept—that is if we are thinking in a dialectical manner."[35] But there was a limit to Sartre's own thinking that came to light once Davis brought race and slavery to bear, for Sartre argued that a slave was free because they could opt between slavery and death. Yet Davis, drawing on the autobiography of Frederick Douglass, as we have done, concluded that this must be false because death represented a final and ultimate retreat from the world. Death represents conceding the right to live in peace and dignity. Thus, no slave was really free until they were liberated. In this way, Davis philosophically pushes our notion of freedom to its limit to show that it is a hollow idea in the hands of those already liberated from white supremacy—namely, white Americans. What blacks need, then, is a conception of freedom rooted in praxis, a conception grounded in and motivated by the visceral notion of liberation as an existential necessity grounded in action and practical reasoning.

Yet, despite her criticism of Sartre, Davis maintains a commitment to the Marx-Sartre axis of critical theory when emphasizing the importance of "authentic consciousness." Just as Marx thought the worker had to come into full consciousness of their historical position under capitalism, Davis says, "The authentic consciousness of an oppressed people entails an understanding of the necessity to abolish oppression. The slave finds at the end of his journey towards understanding a real grasp of what freedom means."[36] And just as Marx thought the condition of the worker under capitalism was a condition of alienation from both themselves and the product of their labor, Davis invites us to consider that "[t]he condition of slavery is a condition of alienation . . . is the absence of authentic identity."[37]

We might accept these propositions yet wonder what work "authentic" is meant to be doing here. What constitutes authentic consciousness and identity? One valuable intervention Davis offers is interrogating or modifying Sartre-Marx by having their ideas confront a different set of problematics contextualized in race and the effects of white supremacy. For as interested in freedom as Sartre or Marx might have been, their theories are indeed color blind, with an unsatisfactory critical consciousness of racial history, of the sins of white supremacy. Davis recalls her initial encounter with Marx: "The *Communist Manifesto* hit me like a bolt of lightning. I read it avidly, finding in it answers to many of the seemingly unanswerable dilemmas which had plagued me."[38] She goes on to say that an attractive idea for her was the possibility that in solving the problems of the proletariat "the foundation was laid for the emancipation of all oppressed peoples."[39] Yet, when the Freedom Rides of 1961 began, Davis did not choose to support factory strikes, for example: "I called my parents to tell them that I wanted to come home [to Birmingham]."[40] I want to suggest that this impulse is the model of authenticity we seek and that Davis offers more assistance in perceiving the nature of authentic consciousness and identity in her later scholarship of blues music.

What is involved in Davis's desire to be a figure in the black struggle, even as she was committed to Marxism and the Communist Party (much as Baraka was committed to Marxism) is a realization much in line with the arguments of her "Lectures on Liberation": that American blackness is not the target of mere economic exploitation. Rather it has been a victim of wholesale existential denigration. White workers might indeed be exploited by the bourgeoisie, but they are still white in a nation founded on whiteness, and, over the course of American history, that is a very great existential advantage. Even poor whites can look at the nation and see themselves as naturally a part of it and at far less danger of summary elimination than any black person, poor or rich. This is what seems to be involved in Davis being committed to the black struggle in America, Marxism notwithstanding. The 1961 Freedom Riders were after far more than fair wages or even the right to vote. Additionally, or maybe more fundamentally, they were fighting for black personhood and black existence. They were endangering their own bodies in seeking to make real a system of liberation wherein blacks could move about the nation, could participate in the nation, make the nation. They and like-minded black Americans understood that the black freedom struggle was one that hinged on blacks' unique historical place in American history and culture—as both essential and endangered, as indispensable and disposable, as culturally coveted in music and art and as politically distasteful in the voting booth or in Congress. This understanding is, I believe, what constitutes for Davis authentic consciousness and identity. And this understanding was powerfully represented by a blues vanguard in the early part of the twentieth century comprised of women.

We have already seen in our discussion of Baraka that the blues, as a genre of music, embodies and is an inheritor of important democratic trademarks as practiced by Africans making work music, and later by slaves working the fields. Also recall that Baraka notes that an important developmental element that gave rise to blues music is the rise of the individual performer, who, early on, might be a traveler, for example. However, this changes when we move from the age of country blues to classic blues. In fact we see two deeply significant shifts that, when combined, must be reckoned as not only an artistic but also a sociopolitical sort of revolution.

First, black women dominated the classic blues scene. This is a fact we will explore a bit more. Second, and I think far less appreciated on its own, and certainly when viewed in the context of the first fact, classic blues arrived at a moment of an immensely significant technological development: recorded music that could be sold for people to listen to in their homes and played on the radio. This gave the nation one of its earliest mass encounters with black artistic brilliance. But it also opened the door to an enduring and, indeed, fraught relationship with American capitalism. The lone country blues artist might wander the country, peppering the nation with their repertoire, which might find a way to stick when other artists picked up the tune, as it were, and went on themselves to perform it. But black women of the classic blues age were the first to establish an archive of the genre. And while there is a worthwhile conversation to be had about the usually problematic economic relationship between the genre and the companies that published the prominent women of the time, I want to draw our attention elsewhere. Namely, I want to use the role of capitalism as a handmaiden to democracy in serving as a conduit, through the selling and distribution of blues records, for expanding the boundaries of American public life. Why is this important?

Davis offers a simple yet crucial observation about the blues: "The blues idiom requires absolute honesty in the portrayal of black life. It is an idiom that does not recognize taboos."[41] Of these taboos we might count the public place of women. A major debate in the 1980s liberal political philosophy, namely in response to John Rawls's *Theory of Justice*, was set by feminist philosophers. These thinkers, Susan Moller Okin prominent among them, took Rawls to task over his omission of the family as part of the basic structural apparatus of developed capitalist democratic societies.[42] This was an important challenge because a key feature of Rawls's theory is its condition that it be conceived of as being for and practiced within a society publicly. By this he meant that it was important that the principles of justice be publicly known to all citizens, that all citizens understand the principles of justice, and all citizens know that all other citizens know the principles of justice. In this way, Rawls imagined achieving a stable conception of justice in theory and then in practice. However, his omission of the family as part of modern society's basic structure relegated the family, historically heteropatriarchal on account of male privilege and domination, to a private sphere where it was seen as nonpolitical, and thus not a site for justice.

Correct as Okin and her colleagues were in pressing the point in the 1980s, black women blues performers were making the same argument roughly a half-century earlier. Davis observes, "The women who sang the blues did not typically affirm female resignation and powerlessness, nor did they accept the segregation of women to private and interior spaces."[43] And even more to the point:

> The performances of the classic blues women—especially Bessie Smith—were one of the few cultural spaces in which a tradition of public discourse on male violence had been previously established. One explanation for the fact that the blues women of the 1920's—and the texts they represent— fail to respect the taboo on speaking publicly about domestic violence is that the blues as a genre never acknowledges the discursive and ideological boundaries separating the private sphere from the public sphere.[44]

One way of absorbing this fact is to see that the blues just was a free-spirited music. But this would be to deny that from its very roots, there were rules and norms to the music that straddled the aesthetic and the ethical. And this would also be to deny the earlier claim that a significant aspect of the roots of blues music from African work songs to the fields was its open and public nature.

Rainey, Smith, and Holiday, then, didn't pioneer the public nature of the blues itself. Rather, they anticipated by many decades the need to bring matters of racial and gender injustice before the public, and this was the value of their partnership with profit-seeking music publishers. Through the wide distribution of their music they were at the same time able to give a voice to matters of sexual abuse and domestic violence. The implied ethic was a model of Rawlsian publicity—they knew, they wanted you to know, and then they wanted you to know that they knew you now knew. As convoluted as that could sound, a brief moment of reflection will reveal to you that this is in fact the very ground of all of our important relationships. We get on with parents, siblings, close friends, or lovers not only when the terms of the relationship are understood by each participant but when each participant is confident that the other person knows the rules and so on. This establishes both trust and, importantly, a foundation to evolve the terms of the relationship.

What the classic blues women laid the foundation for, whether or not through explicit intention, was evolving the social contract with America and doing it through an authentic consciousness, a consciousness in full possession of the varied textures of black life in America. So when Rainey et al. endeavor to speak of what had been typically considered issues of the private sphere, they are both grasping and displaying previously suppressed aspects of that consciousness. This is why Davis frames the importance of the classic black women blues singers within a black feminist context. Though Baraka might have signaled an understanding of the expression of a sexual politics of these women, Davis brings it fully to bear. So when Davis writes, "When women are portrayed as having fulfilled the domestic requirements socially expected of women in relationships with men, it is often to make the point that the women have been abused or abandoned," we see the blues other than through the hazy sepia-romantic lens of early twentieth-century history or, alternatively, merely as the progenitor of jazz, rhythm and blues, or hip-hop.[45] We see the blues as they were meant to be seen—as an ethically laced way of viewing and experiencing the world:

> The blues represent experience as emotionally configured by an individual psyche, historically shaped by post–Civil War conditions and the emancipation of slaves. These conditions are often simply designated as "the blues." The emotional

responses to them are also called "the blues." "The blues" therefore designates both feelings and the circumstances that have provided them.[46]

So now we have an answer to this question: Why was Angela Davis in possession of the gun used by Jonathan Jackson? The answer is: the blues. Clearly, the answer most familiar and expected in response to questions about owning arms will refer to something like self-defense. But let's now think about Davis's first statement of being in proximity to weapons—when she lived on Dynamite Hill and the local whites were determined, by any means necessary, to repulse the wave of black homeowners in their area. Yes, this might seem a straightforward matter of housing segregation, but it is more than that. It is a violation of the public norms of fairness and equality in the pursuit of happiness Americans claim to live by. For blacks, this was usually a lie, a kind of civic deception and betrayal on the basis of little more than an arbitrary decision that black lives, because they were black, did not matter. This is a cause for the blues.

And what of the adult Davis and the gun she owned? By the late 1960s, Davis was fully involved in the struggle for civil rights that was transitioning under Black Power to the struggle for human rights. This had implications for her life. Primary among them was deep insecurity in every way, including, maybe especially, physically. Medgar Evers had been assassinated in 1963; Malcolm X's assassination followed in 1965. King was clearly in danger, and then he was assassinated in 1968. The Chicago-based Black Power leader Fred Hampton seemed similarly marked and was killed the very next year. Additionally, it was also clear to activists that their organizations were being infiltrated by government-sponsored provocateurs. Indeed, this was one of the most urgent reasons Davis was armed.

Davis had become affiliated with the Black Panther Political Party (BPPP) of Los Angeles, which had encountered friction with the presently better-known Black Panther Party for Self-Defense (BPPSD) of Oakland. The BPPSD, led by Huey Newton, at the time from jail, decided to open an office in Los Angeles, and one evening Davis was approached at gunpoint by a man claiming to represent the interests of the BPPSD and demanding that the BPPP change its name. It was a terrifying encounter and not uncommon for others like Davis, who writes, "I could do one of two things—obey him or get my own protection. I chose the latter, and, for a while, was fully armed at all times."[47] The BPPSD learned that the man who threatened Davis was a provocateur, but it didn't matter. Davis had been living the blues. Her nation had been in the historical business of denying her and her people proper personhood, and some blacks, like those at her high school, were susceptible to the rage that governed the ways and means of white supremacy. In this regard, being at the forefront of the 1960s and 1970s freedom struggles, Davis saw the nation as unable to fulfill its promise, neither to itself nor to its darker brethren. The very nature of the collapse of Reconstruction efforts, during which the blues got its first true start, on the roads and porches of America was showing itself to still be a feature of American society, so the blues still had a place there as well.

CONCLUSION

Six days after George Floyd was sent home, Angela Davis illustrated the steadfastness of the relationship between her philosophy and her attitude toward liberation in America. Protests in response to Floyd had grown in size like few in American history. As people, dark and light Americans alike, had been sequestered at home due to the terrifying rise of the COVID-19 pandemic, they had greater exposure to the details of Floyd's public murder, the never-ending media loop of Chauvin's knee on a slowly expiring Floyd. But they also had time, and with that time they took to the streets in greater numbers than at any point in American history. On Davis's view this was because many people previously, in response to the slogan "Black Lives Matter," asked, "'But shouldn't we really be saying all lives matter?' They're now finally getting it. That as long as black people continue to be treated in this way, as long as the violence of racism remains what it is, then no one is safe."[48]

On this view, Davis is consistent with much earlier ideas on the importance of racial justice for all Americans because racial justice gives the entire American project greater integrity. Additionally, she suggests that the philosophical view is justified by the actions of Americans at that moment in support of justice for Floyd.

Initially, this seems right. In the immediate aftermath of Floyd's murder, Black Lives Matter received its strongest public support since its beginning, after Trayvon Martin's death. Yet, the support appeared fickle. Despite the reign of a president sufficiently unashamed of his racism that he more than once expressed sympathy or allyship with white supremacist groups or militias, even liberal Americans seemed unable to sustain extended enthusiasm for Black Lives Matter. Polling data shows that support peaked at 52 percent of respondents in the immediate aftermath of Chauvin's killing Floyd. By January 2021, support had fallen to 47 percent, and by the end of 2021, it was roughly 43 percent. Disturbingly, opposition to Black Lives Matter moved in the exact opposite direction, from 28 percent in the wake of Floyd's death to over 40 percent by the end of 2021.[49]

This might not have surprised Baraka had he been alive; indeed, he likely would have distrusted the nearly spontaneous surge of white sympathy. Though Baraka and Davis both were scholars of the blues, they differed, I think, in how their affection for the music impacted their political outlook, especially with respect to the reliability of white Americans.

However the difference between them on that count works out, one thing I suspect they would agree upon is that the work is far from over. The quest for racial justice has been reinvigorated through the current Black Lives Matter movement, but the fact that we need the movement at all in the twenty-first century, more than sixty years after the successes of the civil rights movement, is deeply concerning. What to do with the simultaneously conflicting but necessary pushes and pulls between hope and wariness? Maybe the greatest lesson from these two thinkers is to retrieve an important part of our cultural heritage and acknowledge that American life for blacks is blues life. This is not a statement that retreats from hope, as the blues is more emotionally capacious and politically astute than commonly accepted. The blues is a source of democratic uplift and provides alternative models to stimulating the civic imagination. But all the same, we might grasp that aspect of the blues and begin to ask, to what project ought we commit ourselves in its name? That is a question for the generations who have to make their way in this land, in the future, but always the home of the blues.

AFTERWORD

Nobody's Protest Essay

IN OUR DAILY PUBLIC DISCOURSE, trolls, voyeurs, schem-
ers, and scammers disrupt conversations that would otherwise contribute to social progress. Such people have as
their main aim the purposeful sabotage of human community, and thus reveal something about their own civic hope-
lessness and soul isolation. But maybe the most unhelpful
people commenting on stories of racial terrorism, or what
mainstream news outlets like to gently call "police shoot-
ings," are the morally dim-witted. I mean that term very literally. To be morally dim-witted is to be a person convinced
of the justice of his or her position yet whose moral perceptions are so deeply mired in racial privilege that the critical perception and judgment needed to correctly interpret
problems is suppressed to the point of motivating asinine
observations and assertions. The harshness of that statement
does nothing to mitigate its truth. Imagine what it is like to
read, as a black person, in the wake of Freddie Gray nearly
losing his head—literally—while in police custody: well, if
he wasn't doing anything wrong, why did he run? As if being
legitimately afraid of the police, in a city where the "Nickel

Ride" is a widely known institution of police abuse, were reason at all to be practically decapitated by the state. Or, more recently with reference to Sandra Bland: why was she acting so arrogantly with the officer by refusing to put out her cigarette? As if asking, with the strong voice of a citizen, why one is being badgered is reason at all to be slammed face first on the ground. The aims of the morally dim-witted are serious. Whereas the trolls et al. maliciously yet helplessly suppress profitable human exchange in the course of making their personal isolation known to the world, the morally dim-witted put on the illusion of profitable exchange by making known to the world their desire to suppress blacks who dare resist the artefacts of racial domination that provide their very social subsistence. They want to make any and all protest a violation of democratic norms, and by some Kafka-esque machination thereby absolve the police and other perpetrators of crimes as serious as murder.

These people—the morally dim-witted—are deeply disturbing, and they are not confined to Internet message boards or forums. They represent a much more significant strand of thinking in America that is eager to proclaim the death of racism even as the black community regularly mourns the death of its young women and men. The everyday morally dim-witted do not only perpetrate wrongs in their own name; they provide cover for many self-satisfied white liberals, who, on account of their more obviously dim-witted counterparts, declare themselves in the moral know and on the political right side of things. But the latter can in fact be more troubling precisely because their self-reflection often extends as far as their sense of righteousness is near to their hearts, which often turns out to be quite near. These people do not want me to live well—the morally dim-witted are unconcerned with my well-being; the self-satisfied are unmotivated to do much to help improve it. I often feel I should hate them, or loathe them. Maybe some of them deserve precisely that sort of response, or what philosophers call that sort of reactive attitude. But it is a tragic truth of our almost-but-not-yet great democracy that embracing the resentment and hatred solves nothing and leaves everything about the very nature of these poor people's poor moral senses unexamined.

When Michael Brown (is said to have) confronted Darren Wilson rather than flee, when Freddie Gray attempted to flee rather than confront, when Sandra Bland spoke up when urged to be silent, we witnessed forms of protest—behaviors, actions, visceral pleas of varying timbres—that signaled to the threatening party (all police officers in these cases) and to us, the witnesses: not today; my dignity is not negotiable today. The person expressing genuine wonder at why anyone would aggressively walk toward, run from, or speak back to abusive authority misses exactly this point. Resistors typically have no interest in challenging authority for the sake of it; rather they seek to preserve the essence of their personhood by, in their own way, enacting a strategy, wisely devised or not, of self-possession. The person who wonders why Sandra Bland spoke back to the cop in question cannot see what Sandra saw—an imminent threat to her personhood. Bland's, and everyone else's death, then, is a false enigma, a puzzle easily solved with the key of white privilege.

The obvious and complete failure of these local and micro-protests reliably results in tragedy, more often than not confirming the mortal frailty of black Americans. When this happens the actions we commonly call protests escalate to take on various forms. In some cases that form is violent and vindictive and one can hardly blame the perpetrators. When one is told so frequently that one's existence is worthless and that its continuation is contingent on the gift-horse kindness of strangers, and then one witnesses gross miscarriages of justice on account of race in the twenty-first century, in a society that supposes itself liberal democratic, well, that is a recipe for resentment of a most explosive sort.

Granting all of this, it's not especially philosophically interesting to ask the rote question, are violent protests ever justified? Hasn't American history already answered that for us in the affirmative? If not, then we had better rethink the grounds for this country's founding and do it quickly, or else it is all an illusion built on a very great crime, history's most prominent and enduring heist. No, whether violent protests are justified is conceptually beside the point, though no doubt a quite live question for representatives of the marginalized on the front lines as well as for those who sincerely intend to keep the peace for peace's sake. The much greater question, and the one that we had better get clear on is this: what rounds out the sharp edges of our rage to keep a grip on the very thing we want to have affirmed and recognized— our humanity?

In his seminal essay "Everybody's Protest Novel," James Baldwin takes egalitarian aim at both white and black authors of the eponymous literary subgenre, the protest novel.[1] For Baldwin, the practitioners of the protest novel make one of two mistakes. Harriet Beecher Stowe dehumanized white perpetrators of admittedly atrocious crimes by reducing them to mere perpetrators: awful persons who enact terrible things that result in horrendous consequences. Richard Wright's Bigger Thomas, who by the end of *Native*

Son reciprocates the history of white supremacists' ire with a vindictive death-dealing spree of his own is reduced to a receptacle of mere rage, racial counterhatred set loose on an unexpecting white readership. Both writers, so far as Baldwin is concerned, commit the sin of forgetting that regardless of how we describe the darkness of white racial hatred or the intense flatness of black revenge, the idea that real people—humans—are behind these actions is occluded by the heavy-handedness of the protest novel. Baldwin wrote, "In overlooking, denying, evading [the human's] complexity . . . we are diminished and we perish; only within this web of ambiguity, paradox, this hunger, danger, darkness, can we find at once ourselves and the power that will free us from ourselves" (13).

We are susceptible to the persuasive pull of facile accounts of human action represented by the kind of protest novel that concerns Baldwin. The reduction of the protagonists to their base motivations comprises "an explanation which falters only if we pause to ask whether or not [Stowe's] picture is indeed complete; and what construction or failure of perception forced her to so depend on the description of brutality . . . and to leave unanswered and unnoticed the only important question: what it was, after all, that moved her people to such deeds" (12). Baldwin thought this a bad way to go for the novelist, since it is his or her prerogative to do the opposite of what is accomplished in these protest novels: interrogate and map the depths of human motivation.

Now, you and I are not trying to puzzle over the appropriate angle of approach for aspiring novelists. Our concern is more immediately political and focused on a society more than fifty years removed from Baldwin's essay. In this society people on the ground are trying to make sense of the persistence of racial hatred that results in what feels like the eternal recurrence of the tragic same. Rage is an understandable and comprehensible response to the parade of atrocities some call American justice. So is demonization of those who benefit from or falsely mourn over those atrocities, or glibly deny the wages of their racial privilege. The fastidiousness of their denials has transformed into a self-pleasuring fetish of a most macabre nature. But we must understand these people.

There are at least three very serious things to understand in our time about these people, most white Americans (though certainly not all). The first very great thing is that they think this is all a game of a sort economists and social scientists identified in the twentieth century: a zero-sum game. People involved in zero-sum games think it is necessarily true that someone else's gain is their loss in the same measure. So if Tyrone gets an extra dollar in wages, they think this necessarily means they must lose a dollar in wages. They think if Kendra receives state support for schooling, this necessarily means their own children will be discriminated against and risk not being adequately educated. They think if the country is asked to mourn and show sympathy for a slain black woman or man, it must necessarily mean that they will, at least, lose favor in their own society, or worse, be the categorical target of retribution and disdain. The list could go on. What is crucial, though, is the mindset in which this puts people. No one who looks at the world this way can be prepared to sacrifice. And here, by sacrifice, I do not mean to lose. Rather, I mean, to make oneself vulnerable to new political possibilities and personal relationships. To loosen the purse strings, to open one's mind and heart means to commit to a change in the civic and economic landscape that one cannot understand until it happens, and when the change comes it will, like all changes, cause all of us to rethink the grounds for our association. It will challenge us to extend thoughts, feelings, and actions in directions we previously thought foreclosed or unwise. This leads to the next thing we must understand.

White Americans have, in one crucial respect, a more acute moral vision than many are prone to credit them with. They know, more surely than black Americans, that the arc of the moral universe bends toward justice. And they know this for two reasons. First, they have been beneficiaries of this profound phenomenon in their own revolutionary struggles. Few doubt the correctness of the French or American revolutions, for example. And we should concede that their successes have left us enduring benefits, not just awful horrors. There is something to be said for a society in which there exists a path to the presidency for a man of Kenyan ancestry. You won't hear me ringing the arrival of a post-racial America, however—Obama's presidency has undoubtedly been marked by some of the most obscene behaviors our nation is capable of producing. Often, it is as if some of our more vicious conservative (and sometimes liberal) counterparts have reached into their bag of Jim Crow tricks to pull out a showstopper of hate and bile. But nonetheless, the path exists—the man won, then he won again, and that simply cannot be ignored.

The second reason white Americans see more clearly than anyone else that the arc of the moral universe bends toward justice is that they have sown the seeds of the undoing of the privilege they so closely covet. On the one hand, they have created and instituted this thing called liberal democracy, and it is a thing that cannot be kept for the select few and maintain its name in even partial good faith. No.

Unless we find ourselves in a clearly authoritarian state, there is always room to fight, and white Americans' hoarding of the civic and economic goods is not lost on them, yet they can do very little to undo the institutions which allow us to fight—no matter how slow or laboriously. Those institutions exist; we must maintain the will. On the other, in those moments when it seems that those institutions will be taken from us, the marginalized, white Americans know they have also set the world a historic example for successful revolution. They know the reasons they threw those cases of tea into the bay on that fateful day, they know why they celebrate Washington's military ingenuity and endurance—freedom and justice are the eternal pillars of a good political society that beckon all those who are prevented from basking in their warmth and security. They know also that history often repeats itself and that their inability to sharpen their moral senses otherwise provides an open invitation for history to return and justify a day of reckoning.

The last thing I want you to understand about many of our white counterparts is that they are afraid, so very afraid. Though they kill us and leave us in the streets, though they lock us in their cages called prisons at disproportionate rates, though they do what they can to box us into the ghettos, they are not as afraid of us in the way these actions often seem to suggest. No, their fear is not a motivation to completely eliminate our presence. Rather, they are afraid to be *without* us in the exact position we are today. Were black Americans to occupy true and genuine equal standing with white Americans, the cachet of being a white American would evaporate before our very eyes. Black Americans must be in a position to constantly plead their worth precisely for white Americans and institutions to affirm their identity as power holders, as the key-bearers of modernity, as those anointed by the Enlightenment. Black Americans must be in a position to constantly demand more wealth precisely for white Americans and institutions to admire their spoils of domination under the guise of hard work and merit. Black Americans must be in a position to constantly prove their competence in the halls of excellence, wherever they be, in order to substantiate white Americans' sense of expertise and fundamental knowledge. For all these reasons white Americans are more afraid of equality than they are of us because equality provides a more enduring threat to who they are than a kid in a hoodie.

I say all this because our moment demands equality, while every fresh news cycle invites us to be caught up in our own passions, desires, longings, and rages. I have felt this pull and I cannot honestly say I have freed myself from it. All of these feelings are warranted, there can be no question about that. We are all of us human, and to see the person who could be you die in a manner that recalls Emmett Till's face beaten and bloated as much by hatred as by the river waters that overtook his biology, who is anyone to tell you to not rage, to not want to throw a brick through that window? Maybe these are things that blacks will ultimately have to do anyway— remember, seizing liberty from the hands of the reticent is this nation's patrimony. But however we fight the good fight, we must not lose sight of how complex humans are, even those who with all your heart you feel will never do you any good. The very greatest burden on black Americans today is the need to balance hope for an uncertain future against the rage they feel here and now over a crime you yourself witnessed while eating dinner but that the courts declared was business as usual. This burden is the business of being human, even if blacks find themselves holding the bum lottery ticket of political history. However, we are humans holding that lottery ticket and the duty to hope is real because our humanity is the very thing we insist on being recognized at every turn: in the courts, in the classroom, in the boardroom, in the welfare office, at the bank loan officer's desk, in the doctor's office, and everywhere else. If our hope only takes on the form of rage made manifest in the world, then it is really only a chimera that suits itself to the needs of the media agencies and the expectations of those who need you where you are. That cannot be the hope that defines a people, nor is it the kind that moves a mountain of oppression. It invites its own illegitimacy and renders all protest as so much commotion. As unfair the burden, I hope that we can see that. Otherwise, this is nobody's protest essay.

JUST ONE MORE THING

A struggle is only beautiful if you find yourself on the winning side when it's all over. I don't mean the kind of struggles that one experiences periodically, at particular moments of inconvenience or even injustice. I mean, struggle against the kinds of things that day in and day out will shape your life—you wake up and are sad because of it; you wake up and are happy despite it. But however it shakes out, the struggle intrudes upon your life and the worst part is, you didn't put it there in the first place.

This dynamic is a great burden and we have ways of dealing with it. I write—that is one of my ways, and a main way. We are all taught early on, beginning in grade school, and then through graduate school, and then by our editors (if these last two apply): imagine your audience and write to them. My own experience is that when I've written with this mantra explicitly in mind, I've done my worst writing. To be clear, the writing—the prose—itself might have been executed quite well. But I was usually not the most honest I could and ought to have been. The struggle in that instance is not only not beautiful, but it also is not a means to victory.

When I write at my best, I am not writing to you—I am writing to me for you. I'm sorry, but I'm too busy with the struggle to be much concerned with whether you agree with me. I sometimes don't even agree with myself in an unqualified sense. But I am trying to save myself. The struggle of life in this country is a lot to bear. Some do it gallantly, some do it with stoicism, some do it shedding a tear in a quiet corner when no one is looking, or when he thinks no one is looking. But I see him—he's using the corner I used some long time ago; may it serve him well. I am neither gallant nor stoic—and I refuse to be made to shed any more tears that haven't been earned though mutual affection and embrace. When I say I am trying to save myself when I write, I am saying this—I am constructing a different space, away from the weeping corner, where I might stand as a human being demanding the recognition that deserves. It is a place where my dignity is holy and my autonomy is inviolable. You cannot do anything to me when I stand there. When I write to me, to save myself, for you I am clearing a space for you to stand with me and it is really entirely up to you whether you stand there, too. True, maybe the invitation misfires from time to time, but be honest—you've gotten invitations with the wrong address printed on them, and that never stopped you from trying to get into the party anyway. Why would you complain now?

This body of prose, "Nobody's Protest Essay," is a struggle within myself to not write you off—all of you, all colors and creeds, because to be honest, I am quite tired of this thing I see on the news, on the streets, in the paper, on the Internet, in institutions, at dinner parties—the inhumanity of it all played out in varying registers from the tragicomic to the operatic just because I/we were born. That is our only crime, and it is only a crime because we are punished for breathing. "The pen is mightier than the sword"—maybe, maybe not. But I do know that words can form somewhat useful shields and even remarkably useful mirrors. But no mirror has been useful without someone willing to gaze in it.

The most likely misreading of this essay—and likely due to some fault in my presentation—is that I am ultimately calling for black Americans to turn the other cheek, but really, nothing could be farther from the truth. Rather, it is me trying to make my anger more intelligent and precise, and nothing has ever been more destabilizing to the status quo than that—the discipline to smile to keep a conversation going just so you may ultimately win the argument rather than storm off without the goods you came for in the first place; and the discipline to stop smiling when it really is the case that you thought you came to argue, when the other person thought you came to beg on bended knee. If the discipline is well-honed then we also come to realize when it's really revolution time, which is something quite opposite from turning the other cheek. And, yes, it can tell us also when it's peace and forgiveness time. Neither stance is intrinsically superior—in a complex political world populated by both the reasonable and the intransigent the question is always, which more genuinely secures the integrity of our personhood? This is one aspect of my struggle and I've tried to clear a space for you to stand with me. We are not in the corner and our backs are not up against a wall. We are free to move how we want so we should make the most of it, with charity and grace.

NOTES

Introduction to the Updated Edition

1. Matthew Singer, "Portland's 'Naked Athena' Speaks for the First Time to a Local Podcase," *Willamette Week*, July 26, 2020, https://www.wweek.com/news/2020/07/26/portlands-naked-athena-speaks-for-the-first-time-to-local-podcast/.
2. "Black Lives Matter Registered Voters, April 25, 2017–October 11, 2022," CIVIQS, accessed October 12, 2022. https://civiqs.com/results/black_lives_matter?annotations=true&uncertainty=true&zoomIn=true.

Introduction

1. "The Creation of a Movement," *Black Lives Matter, a Herstory of the #BlackLivesMatter Movement*, newsletter, n.d., accessed October 23, 2016, http://blacklivesmatter.com/herstory/.

Chapter 1

1. Which is not to say that the exploitation of black bodies for labor had disappeared. Indeed, it reappeared in troubling

ways, such as in prisons. See Douglas A. Blackmon, *Slavery by Another Name: The Re-Enslavement of Black Americans from the Civil War to World War II* (New York: Anchor, 2009).

2. Frederick Douglass, "The Union and How to Save It," in *Selected Speeches and Writings*, edited by Philip S. Foner (Chicago: Lawrence Hill Books, 1999), 429–31.

3. Frederick Douglass, "*Narrative of a Life*," in *Douglass: Autobiographies* (New York: Library of America, 1994), 1–102, at 15. For a very interesting and helpful analysis of the evolution of Douglass's analytic and writing style across the three autobiographies, see Robert S. Levine, *The Lives of Frederick Douglass* (Cambridge, MA: Harvard University Press, 2016).

4. For an interesting perspective on the philosophical relationship between Douglass's fight with Covey and his work as an abolitionist, see Frank M. Kirklan, "Is an Existential Reading of the Fight with Covey Sufficient to Explain Frederick Douglass's Critique of Slavery?," *Critical Philosophy of Race* 3, no. 1 (2015): 124–51.

5. For an extended discussion on the philosophical uses of shame for Douglass, see Bernard R. Boxill, "Fear and Shame as Forms of Moral Suasion in the Thought of Frederick Douglass," *Transactions of the Charles S. Peirce Society* 31, no. 3 (1995): 713–44.

6. Frederick Douglass, "What, to the Slave, Is the Fourth of July?," in *Great Speeches by African-Americans*, edited by James Baley (New York: Dover, 2006), 13–34, at 16–17.

7. This is in part accomplished by, as Jason Frank terms it, "staging dissensus." See Jason Frank, "Staging Dissensus: Frederick Douglass and 'We, the People,'" in *Law and Agonistic Politics*, ed. Andrew Schaap (Farnham: Ashgate, 2009), 87–104.

8. Douglass, "What to the Slave?," 25–26.

9. Frederick Douglass, "The Constitution of the United States: Is It Pro-Slavery or Antislavery?," in *Frederick Douglass: Selected Speeches and Writings*, edited by Richard S. Foner (Chicago: Lawrence Hill Books, 1975), 380–90, at 380.

10. Ibid., 381.

11. Douglass, "Government and Its Subjects," in Foner, *Frederick Douglass* 146–48, at 147.

12. Douglass, "To Thomas Auld," in Foner, *Frederick Douglass*, 111–16, at 113.
13. There is also the interesting question of the role of the sentiment in Douglass's writings. See Stephanie A. Smith, "Heart Attacks: Frederick Douglass's Strategic Sentimentality," *Criticism* 34, no. 2 (1992): 193–216.
14. Douglass, "To Thomas Auld," in Foner, *Frederick Douglass*, 111–16, at 116.
15. Douglass, "To Capt. Thomas Auld, Formerly My Master," in Foner, *Frederick Douglass*, 143–45, at 144.
16. Frederick Douglass, in Ida B. Wells, "A Red Record", *The Light of Truth: Writings of an Anti-Lynching Crusader*, edited and with an introduction by Mia Bay (New York: Penguin, 2014), 218–312, at 218.
17. *Crusade for Justice: The Autobiography of Ida B. Wells*, edited by Afreda M. Duster (Chicago: University of Chicago Press, 1970), 47.
18. John Dilulio, "The Coming of the Superpredators," in *National Review*, November 27, 1995.
19. Wells, "Southern Horrors: Lynch Law in All Its Phases," in *Light of Truth*, 77.
20. Patricia A. Schechter, *Ida B. Wells-Barnett and American Reform 1880–1930* (Chapel Hill: University of North Carolina Press, 2001), 84.
21. Wells, "Lynch Law and the Color Line," in *Light of the Truth*, 122.
22. Wells, "How Enfranchisement Stops Lynchings," in *Light of the Truth*, 424.
23. For an insightful analysis of the role of subjectivity and commentary on lynchings in both journalism and literature, see Jean M. Lutes, "Lynching Coverage and the American Reporter-Novelist," *American Literary History* 19, no. 2 (Summer 2007): 456–81.
24. Wells, "Lynch Law and the Color Line," in *Light of Truth*, 121.
25. Jacqueline Goldsby, *A Spectacular Secret: Lynching in American Life and Literature* (Chicago: University of Chicago Press, 2006), 101.
26. Wells, "The Requirements of Southern Journalism," in *Light of the Truth*, 91.

27. Michael C. Dawson, *Behind the Mule: Race and Class in African-American Politics* (Princton, NJ: Princeton University Press, 1995).
28. Richard H. McAdams, *The Expressive Powers of Law: Theories and Limits* (Cambridge, MA: Havard University Press, 2015).
29. Jason Henry, "'Lynching' Laws Were Meant to Protect Black People: Removing the Word Changed Everything," *Pasadena Star-News*, website, June 11, 2016, updated June 13, 2016, accessed October 23, 2016, http://www.pasadenastarnews. com/government-and-politics/20160611/lynching-laws-were-meant-to-protect-black-people-removing-the-word-changed-everything.

Chapter 2

1. It might seem to readers that the Harlem Renaissance was a more or less coherent or monolithic era in black culture. It wasn't. Nor do I mean to suggest as much. Rather, I want to highlight some of the main currents that seem fairly prominent and important for our purposes. For an excellent discussion of divisions and intrigue among the principals of the era, see George Hutchinson, *The Harlem Renaissance in Black and White* (Cambridge, MA: Belknap Press, 1995), esp. chap. 13.
2. David Levering Lewis. *When Harlem Was in Vogue* (New York: Penguin, 1997).
3. James Weldon Johnson, "Harlem: The Cultural Capital," in *The New Negro: Voices of the Harlem Renaissance*, ed. Alain Locke (New York: Simon and Schuster, 1992), 301–11, at 301–2.
4. Alain Locke, "The New Negro," in *The New Negro: Voices of the Harlem Renaissance*, edited by Alain Locke (New York: Touchstone, 1992), 3–18, at 10.
5. Ibid., 11.
6. Ibid., 8–9.
7. Ibid., 9.
8. Ibid., 15.
9. Jeffrey C. Stewart, "The New Negro as Citizen," in *The Cambridge Companion to the Harlem Renaissance*, ed. George

Hutchinson (New York: Cambridge University Press, 2007), 13–27, at 20.

10. Langston Hughes, *Selected Letters of Langston Hughes*, edited by Arnold Rampersad and David Roessel, with Christa Fratantoro (New York: A. A. Knopf, 2015), 23.

11. Langston Hughes, "The Negro Speaks of Rivers," in *The Collected Poems of Langston Hughes*, edited by Arnold Rampersad (New York: Vintage, 1994), 22.

12. Ibid.

13. Langston Hughes, "The Negro Artist and the Racial Mountain," in *The Portable Harlem Renaissance Reader*, edited by David Levering Lewis (New York: Penguin Books), 91–95, at 92.

14. Though Hughes's relationship to "primitivism" was more problematic. See David Chinitz, "Rejuvenation through Joy: Langston Hughes, Primitivism, and Jazz," *American Literary History* 9, no. 1 (1997): 60–78.

15. Hughes, note 13, 92.

16. Ibid.

17. Ibid., 94.

18. Langston Hughes, "The Weary Blues," in *The Weary Blues* (New York: Alfred Knopf, 2015), 5–6, at 5.

19. Langston Hughes, "I, Too," in *Collected Poems*, 46.

20. Ibid.

21. Ibid.

22. Hazel Carby, *Reconstructing Womanhood: The Emergence of the Afro-American Woman Novelist* (New York: Oxford University Press, 1987), 166.

23. Zora Neal Hurston, "How It Feels to Be Colored Me," in *Hurston: Folklore, Memoirs, and Other Writings* (New York: Library of America), 829 (emphasis in original).

24. Ibid., 827. Hurston's attitude oddly morphed into what many consider a tragic conservatism during the *Brown v. Board* years. See Andrew Delbanco, "The Political Incorrectness of Zora Neale Hurston," *Journal of Black in Higher Education*, 18 (Winter 1997–98): 103–8. Prior to those years, however, a separate issue was that Hurston's attitude was unorthodox for a woman and seemed to earn her biased treatment from her peers. See Ralph D. Story, "Gender and Ambition: Zora

Neale Hurston in the Harlem Renaissance," in *Black Scholar* 20, no. 3/4 (1989): 25–31.

25. Hurston, "The 'Pet Negro' System," in *Hurston*, 917.
26. Zora Neale Hurston, *Zora Neale Hurston: A Life in Letters*, ed. Carla Kaplan (New York: Anchor Books, 2005), 116.
27. Paul Allen Anderson, *Deep River: Music and Memory in Harlem Renaissance Thought* (Durham, NC: Duke University Press, 2001), 199.
28. Anthea Kraut, *Choreographing the Folk: The Dance Stagings of Zora Neale Hurston* (Minneapolis: Minnesota University Press, 2008), 65.
29. Hurston, "Crazy for This Democracy," in *Hurston*, 948.
30. Geraldo Rivera. Newscast. *The Five*, Fox News. June 30, 2015.

Chapter 3

1. Leonard Buder, "Officers' Union Runs Ads Backing Action of Police in Bumpurs Case," *New York Times*, website, December 13, 1984, accessed October 23, 2016, http://www.nytimes.com/1984/12/13/nyregion/officers-union-runs-ads-backing-action-of-police-in-bumpurs-case.html.
2. Anna Julia Cooper, "A Voice from the South," in *The Voice of Anna Julia Cooper*, ed. by Charles Lemert and Esme Bahan (New York: Rowman and Littlefield, 1998), 51–196, at 62 (emphasis in original).
3. Vivian M. May, *Anna Julia Cooper, Visionary Black Feminist* (New York: Routledge, 2012), 13.
4. For a penetrating analysis of the history of black activism and thought centering on the work of black men, see Hazel Carby, *Race Men* (Cambridge, MA: Harvard University Press, 1998).
5. Beverly Guy-Sheftall provides a very useful overview of the academy's rediscovery and reclamation of Cooper's work in "Black Feminist Studies: The Case of Anna Julia Cooper," *African American Review* 43, no. 1 (Spring 2009): 11–15.
6. See Michel Foucault, *Discipline and Punish: The Birth of the Prison*, trans. Alan Sheridan (New York: Vintage, 1995).

7. Cooper, "Woman versus the Indian," in Lemert and Behan, *The Voice*, 91.

8. Ibid., 92.

9. Elizabeth Alexander emphasizes both Cooper's powers as an intellectual and the distinctiveness her personal experiences lent her intellectualism, in "'We Must Be about Our Father's Business': Anna Julia Cooper and the In-Corporation of the Nineteenth Century African-American Woman Intellectual," *Signs* 20, no. 2 (Winter 1995): 336–56. See also Vivian M. May, "Writing the Self into Being: Anna Julia Cooper's Textual Politics," *African American Review*, 43 no. 1 (Spring 2009): 17–34.

10. Booker T. Washington, "The Atlanta Exposition Address," in *Great Speeches by African-Americans*, edited by James Daly (Mineola, NY: Dover, 2006), 81–84, at 83.

11. May, *Visionary Black Feminist*, 25.

12. Anna Julia Cooper, "Equality of Race and the Democratic Movement," in *Voice of Anna Julia Cooper*, 291–98, at 296–97.

13. Cooper has also, in more recent times, been charged with being elitist, alongside fellow thinkers such as W. E. B. Du Bois. See Cathryn Bailey, "Anna Julia Cooper, 'Dedicated in the Name of My Slave Mother to the Education of Colored Working People," *Hypatia* 19, no. 2 (Spring 2004): 56–73.

14. Cooper, "Voice from the South," 63.

15. Audre Lorde, "Who Said It Was Simple?," in *The Collected Poems of Audre Lorde* (New York: W. W. Norton, 1997), 92.

16. For a reading of Lorde as responding to the narratives and myths that attend patriarchy, see Ann Louise Keating, "Making 'Our Shattered Faces Whole': The Black Goddess and Audre Lorde's Revision of Patriarchal Myth," *Frontiers: A Journal of Women Studies* 13, no. 1 (1992): 20–33.

17. Audre Lorde, *Zami, A New Spelling of My Name: A Biomythography* (New York: Crossing Press, 1982), 15.

18. Ibid.

19. Audre Lorde, "There Is No Hierarchy of Oppression," in *I Am Your Sister: Collected and Unpublished Writings of Audre Lorde*, ed. by Rudolph Byrd, Johnetta Betsch Cole, and Beverly

Guy-Sheftall (New York: Oxford University Press, 2009), 219–20, at 219.

20. For a discussion of the role writing and expression played in self-possession for Lorde, see Margaret Kissam Morris, "Audre Lorde: Textual Authority and the Embodied Self," *Frontiers: A Journal of Women Studies* 23, no. 1 (2002): 168–88.

21. Audre Lorde, "Uses of the Erotic: The Erotic as Power," in *Sister Outsider: Essays and Speeches by Audre Lorde* (Berkeley: Crossing Press, 2007), 53–59, at 53. See also Ruth Ginzberg, "Audre Lorde's (Nonessentialist) Lesbian Eros," *Hypatia* 7, no. 4 (Autumn 1993): 73–90; and Anh Hua, "Audre Lorde's *Zami*, Erotic Embodies Memory, and the Affirmation of Difference," *Frontiers: A Journal of Women Studies* 36, no. 1 (2015): 113–35.

22. Lorde, "Uses of the Erotic," in *Sister Outsider*, 57.

23. Audre Lourde, "Sadomasochism: Not about Condemnation," in *I Am Your Sister*, 52.

24. Ibid. See also Lynn S. Chancer, *Sadomasochism in Everyday Life: The Dynamics of Power and Powerlessness* (New Brunswick, NJ: Rutgers University Press, 1992); and Lynn S. Chancer, *Pornography: The Production and Consumption of Inequality*, edited by Gail Dines, Bob Jensen, and Ann Russo (New York: Routledge, 1997).

25. Lorde, "No Hierarchy of Oppression," in *I Am Your Sister*, 220.

26. Alicia Garza, "A Herstory of the #BlackLivesMatter Movement," in *The Feminist Wire*, October 7, 2014, accessed Nov. 22, 2016. http://www.thefeministwire.com/2014/10/blacklivesmatter-2/.

Chapter 4

1. Mark Berman, "'I Forgive You': Relatives of Charleston Church Shooting Victims Address Dylann Roof," *Washington Post*, June 19, 2015, accessed October 22, 2016, https://www.washingtonpost.com/news/post-nation/wp/2015/06/19/i-forgive-you-relatives-of-charleston-church-victims-address-dylann-roof/?utm_term=.87e9e9e1e6ae.

2. The Riverbends Channel. "James Baldwin Debates William F. Buckley (1965). Online video clip. YouTube. 27 October 2012. Web. Accessed Nov 22, 2016.

3. David Leeming, *James Baldwin: A Biography* (New York: Henry Holt, 1994), 24.

4. James Baldwin, "The Harlem Ghetto," in *Baldwin: Collected Essays* (New York: Library of America, 1998), 42–53, at 53.

5. James Baldwin, "No Name in the Street," in *Baldwin: Collected Essays*, 349–476, at 357.

6. James Baldwin, "The Fire Next Time," in *Baldwin: Collected Essays*, 291–348, at 291.

7. Baldwin, note 6, 302.

8. Ibid., 298.

9. Ibid., 309.

10. Ibid., 293.

11. Ibid., 294.

12. James Baldwin, "A Report from Occupied Territory," in *Baldwin: Collected Essays*, 722–38, at 734.

13. Baldwin, "Fire Next Time," 321.

14. James Baldwin, "Nobody Knows My Name," in *Baldwin: Collected Essays*, 137–290, at 142.

15. James Baldwin, "The Last Interview (with Quincy Troupe)," in *James Baldwin: The Last Interview; and Other Conversations* (New York: Melville House Publishing), 88.

16. Stephen B. Oates, *Let the Trumpet Sound: A Life of Martin Luther King, Jr.* (New York: Harper Perennial, 1982), 362.

17. James Baldwin, "The Dangerous Road before Martin Luther King," in *Baldwin: Collected Essays*, 638–58, at 639.

18. Taylor Branch, *Parting the Waters: America in the King Years 1954-1963* (New York: Simon and Schuster, 1988), 75.

19. Martin Luther King Jr., "Kenneth B. Clark Interview," in *A Testament of Hope: Essential Writings of Martin Luther King, Jr.*, edited by James M. Washington (New York: HarperCollins, 1986), 331–39, at 334.

20. Ibid., 335.

21. Martin Luther King Jr., "An Experiment in Love," in *Testament of Hope*, 16–20, at 17.

22. Ibid., 19.

23. Ibid., 19.
24. Ibid., 18.
25. Martin Luther King Jr., "The Power of Nonviolence," in *Testament of Hope*, 12–15, at 12–13.
26. Baldwin, "Fire Next Time," 304.

Chapter 5

1. Thomas Sowell, "Too Many Apologies," in *The Dismantling of America* (New York: Basic Books, 2010), 240–42, at 240.
2. Sowell, "Taking America for Granted," in *Dismantling of America*, 195–97, at 195.
3. Randall Kennedy, "Lifting as We Climb," *Harper's Magazine*, October 2015, accessed October 24, 2016, http://harpers.org/archive/2015/10/lifting-as-we-climb/2/.
4. Cooper, "Voice from the South," 63.
5. Glenn Loury, "Loury: The Political Inefficacy of Saying 'Black Lives Matter,'" op ed., *Brown Daily Herald*, November 6, 2015, accessed October 24, 2016, http://www.browndailyherald.com/2015/11/06/loury-the-political-inefficacy-of-saying-black-lives-matter/.
6. Lorde, "No Hierarchy of Oppression," in *I Am Your Sister*, 220.
7. John McWhorter, *Winning the Race: Beyond the Crisis in Black America* (New York: Gotham Books, 2006), 7.
8. Michelle Alexander, *The New Jim Crow: Mass Incarceration in the Age of Colorblindness* (New York: New Press, 2012).

Chapter 6

1. See, for example, Nicholas Bogel-Burroughs and Will Wright, "Little Has Been Said about the $20 Bill That Brought Officers to the Scene," *New York Times*, April 19, 2021, https://www.nytimes.com/2021/04/19/us/george-floyd-bill-counterfeit.html.
2. Friedrich Nietzsche, *The Gay Science*, trans. Walter Kaufmann (New York: Vintage, 1974).
3. Amiri Baraka, *Blues People: Negro Music in White America* (New York: Harper Perennial, 2002), 8.

4. Angela Davis, *Blues Legacies and Black Feminism: Gertrude "Ma" Rainey, Bessie Smith, and Billie Holiday* (New York: Vintage Books, 1999), 7.

5. For a modest sampling of a large and growing literature on various aspects of the Black Power movement/era, see the following: select essays in Dayo F. Gure, Jeanne Theoharis, and Komozi Woodard, eds., *Want to Start a Revolution: Radical Women in the Black Freedom Struggle* (New York: New York University Press, 2009); Peniel Joseph, *Waiting 'til the Midnight Hour: A Narrative History of Black Power in America* (New York: Henry Holt, 2006); Huey P. Newton, *Revolutionary Suicide* (New York: Penguin Books, 1973); Bettye Collier-Thomas and V. P. Franklin, eds., *Sisters in the Struggle: African American Women in the Civil Rights–Black Power Movement* (New York: New York University Press, 2001); Joshua Bloom and Waldo E. Martin Jr., *Black against Empire: The History and Politics of the Black Panther Party* (Berkeley: University of California Press, 2013); Martha Biondi, *The Black Revolution on Campus* (Berkeley: University of California Press, 2012).

6. Kwame Ture and Charles V. Hamilton, *Black Power: The Politics of Liberation in America* (New York: Vintage Books, 1967), ix (emphasis in original).

7. Here is W. E. B. Du Bois describing his moment of developing a two-ness during a card exchange at school during his youth: "I remember well when the shadow swept across me. . . . The exchange was merry, till one girl, a tall newcomer, refused my card. . . . Then it dawned on me with a certain suddenness that I was different from the others[.]" *The Souls of Black Folk*, ed. Henry Louis Gates and Terri Hume Oliver (New York: W. W. Norton, 1999), 10.

8. Amiri Baraka, *The Autobiography of Leroi Jones* (Chicago: Lawrence Hill Books, 1984), 39.

9. Ibid.

10. Ibid., 41.

11. Ibid., 83.

12. Robert Palmer, *Deep Blues* (New York: Penguin Books, 1981), 28.

13. John Rawls, *A Theory of Justice* (Cambridge, MA; Belknap Press, 1999).
14. See especially section II of Karl Marx, "The Communist Manifesto," in *The Marx-Engels Reader,* 2nd edition, ed. Robert C. Tucker (New York: W. W. Norton, 1978), 469–500.
15. Baraka, *The Autobiography,* 244.
16. Ibid., 245.
17. Leroi Jones, *Dutchman & The Slave* (New York: Harper Perennial, 2001), 12 (emphasis in original).
18. Ibid., 35.
19. It might be more than mere naming coincidence, thus serendipitous, in support of my claim that the American Blues Theater staged a version of *Dutchman* in its thirty-first season, August 26–September 25, 2016. "Dutchman/Transit," American Blues Theater, accessed October 12, 2022, https://americanbluestheater.com/season-31/dutchmantransit/.
20. James Smethurst, *Brick City Vanguard: Amiri Baraka, Black Music, Black Modernity* (Amherst: University of Massachusetts Press, 2020), 59.
21. Ibid.
22. Ibid., 60.
23. Amiri Baraka, *Blues People: Negro Music in White America* (New York: Harper Perennial, 2002), 1.
24. Ibid., 20.
25. Palmer, *Deep Blues,* 29.
26. Baraka, *Blues People,* 62.
27. Coltrane had lived a life marked by addiction, and in confronting that demon, as is often the case, he opened the door to believe in a higher power to which he was grateful.
28. Baraka, *Blues People,* 91.
29. In addition to some suggestions above, see also Robyn C. Spencer, *The Revolution Has Come: Black Power, Gender, and the Black Panther Party in Oakland* (Durham, NC: Duke University Press, 2016); Catherine Morris and Rujeko Hockley, eds., *We Wanted a Revolution: Black Radical Women 1965–85: A Sourcebook* (New York: Brooklyn Museum, 2017). For a more intimate, biographical exploration, see Elaine Brown, *A Taste of Power: A Black Woman's Story* (New York: Anchor Books, 1992).

30. George Jackson, *Soledad Brother* (Chicago: Lawrence Hill Books, 1994). The significance of the title was that Jackson was one of three men serving time in Soledad Prison for charges linked to the death of a guard in a prison uprising.

31. Angela Davis, *Angela Davis: An Autobiography* (New York: International Publishers, 1974), 78.

32. Ibid., 100.

33. Angela Davis, "Lectures on Freedom," N.Y. Committee to Free Angela Davis, New York, 1971. p. 3.

34. For example, see Jean-Paul Sartre, *Being and Nothingness: An Essay on Phenomenological Ontology*, trans. Sarah Richmond (New York: Washington Square Press, 2021).

35. Davis, "Lectures on Freedom," 4.

36. Ibid., 5.

37. Ibid., 6–7.

38. Davis, *An Autobiography*, 109.

39. Ibid., 110.

40. Ibid., 112.

41. Davis, *Blues Legacies*, 107.

42. Susan Moller Okin, *Justice, Gender, and the Family* (New York: Basic Books, 1991).

43. Davis, *Blues Legacies*, 20.

44. Ibid., 25.

45. Ibid., 17.

46. Ibid., 112.

47. Davis, *An Autobiography*, 164.

48. Lanre Bakare, "Angela Davis: 'We Knew That the Role of the Police Was to Protect White Supremacy,'" *The Guardian*, June 15, 2020, https://www.theguardian.com/us-news/2020/jun/15/angela-davis-on-george-floyd-as-long-as-the-violence-of-racism-remains-no-one-is-safe.

49. "Black Lives Matter Registered Voters."

Afterword

1. Baldwin, "Everybody's Protest Novel," in *James Baldwin: Collected Essays*, 11–18.

INDEX